Research &
Education
Association

Math
Review
for the *SAT*

The Staff of Research & Education Association

Research & Education Association
Visit our website at
www.rea.com

Research & Education Association
61 Ethel Road West
Piscataway, New Jersey 08854
E-mail: info@rea.com

MATH REVIEW FOR THE SAT

Pubished 2009

Printed in the United States of America

Library of Congress Control Number 2005931096

ISBN 13: 978-0-7386-0086-4
ISBN 10: 0-7386-0086-5

CONTENTS

ABOUT RESEARCH & EDUCATION ASSOCIATION

Founded in 1959, Research & Education Association is dedicated to publishing the finest and most effective educational materials—including software, study guides, and test preps—for students in middle school, high school, college, graduate school, and beyond.

REA's Test Preparation series includes books and software for all academic levels in almost all disciplines. Research & Education Association publishes test preps for students who have not yet entered high school, as well as high school students preparing to enter college. Students from countries around the world seeking to attend college in the United States will find the assistance they need in REA's publications. For college students seeking advanced degrees, REA publishes test preps for many major graduate school admission examinations in a wide variety of disciplines, including engineering, law, and medicine. Students at every level, in every field, with every ambition can find what they are looking for among REA's publications.

REA's practice tests are always based upon the most recently administered exams, and include every type of question that can be expected on the actual exams.

REA's publications and educational materials are highly regarded and continually receive an unprecedented amount of praise from professionals, instructors, librarians, parents, and students. Our authors are as diverse as the fields represented in the books we publish. They are well-known in their respective disciplines and serve on the faculties of prestigious high schools, colleges, and universities throughout the United States and Canada.

We invite you to visit us at *www.rea.com* to find out how "REA is making the world smarter."

ACKNOWLEDGMENTS

In addition to our authors, we would like to thank Larry B. Kling, Vice President, Editorial, for his overall direction; Pam Weston, Vice President, Publishing, for setting the quality standards for production integrity and managing the publication to completion; Christine Reilley, Senior Editor, for project management and preflight editorial review; Stacey Farkas, Senior Editor, and Jeanne Audino, Senior Editor, for editorial contributions; Diane Goldschmidt, Associate Editor, for post-production quality assurance; Edward Bonny, Copywriter, for editorial contributions; Christine Saul, Senior Graphic Artist, for designing the cover; and Jeff LoBalbo, Senior Graphic Artist, for post-production file mapping.

We also gratefully acknowledge the team at Publication Services for page composition.

GETTING THE MOST OUT OF YOUR MATH REVIEW

THE SAT AND THIS BOOK

We know that the math part of the SAT looms as one of the most difficult and challenging parts of the entire college admissions process. If that includes you, this book will ease your mind.

With the coming of every year, a new crop of students prepares for the SAT. In bookstores, online, and in libraries, they face an untold number of SAT preparation books, with each one claiming to offer new, unbeatable strategies or to have somehow solved the SAT. Strategies can be vital test tools but they are not infallible guides. The SAT is not a mystery that needs to be cracked open but rather a known quantity that needs to be mastered.

The fact is, there are no instant answers or pat solutions when it comes to taking the SAT.

That's where this book comes in. Think of it as your personal Math tutor for the SAT. It is intended to aid you significantly in preparing for the Multiple-Choice and Student-Produced Response sections of the SAT. By studying with this book, you will learn how to work through SAT problems by applying simple, systematic rules to enable you to reach the right answers.

The practice problems you will find inside this book have been thoughtfully patterned after the actual SAT. Each answer is fully explained to provide you with a greater understanding of what the SAT expects from you.

You'll find this book to be perfect for self-guided study. Open it up anywhere and any time you are free to answer even just one question—on the bus, waiting on line in the cafeteria, or even between classes. The more you work at it, the more your skills will improve.

Understanding SAT Math: Subject Areas

As you proceed through this book, you will learn to identify the types of questions that appear on the math section of the SAT. Part I reviews the Multiple-Choice Section. Part II covers the Student-Produced Response Section. Both parts cover four major subject areas: numbers and operations; algebra and functions; geometry and measurement; and data analysis, statistics, and probability. The SAT includes such subjects as linear functions, manipulations with exponents, properties of tangent lines, exponential growth, absolute value, and functional notation. Once you have completed the book, you will have gained a deeper understanding of all the mathematics questions that are tested on the SAT.

FORMAT OF THE SAT

Each of the three test sections—Reading, Writing, and Math—is scored using a 200–800 scale, making 2400 the highest score possible. The total testing time is 3 hours and 20 minutes.

Mathematics Sections: 70 minutes

In the Mathematics sections, you will encounter the following question types that test your algebra, arithmetic, geometry, and data analysis skills:

- Multiple choice: 44 multiple-choice questions that test your general math knowledge.

- Student-Produced Response: 10 questions requiring you to solve problems and then enter your answers onto the provided grid. There are no multiple-choice answers in this section.

The following chart summarizes the format of the Math section of the SAT.

Section	Content	Item Type	Time	Score
Math	• Number and operations • Algebra (now including Algebra II) and functions • Geometry and measurement • Statistics, probability, and data analysis	• Five-choice multiple-choice questions • Student-produced responses (which you may know as grid-ins)	70 min. total (previously 75 min.): two 25-min. sections and one 20-min. section	200-800

ON THE USE OF CALCULATORS

Although solutions can be found to every math problem without them, calculators are permitted during the SAT. You may use a programmable or nonprogrammable four-function, scientific, or graphing calculator. Pocket organizers, handheld mini PCs, PDAs, paper tape, noisy calculators, and calculators requiring an external power source are not allowed. Sharing calculators is not permitted.

ABOUT THE TEST

Who takes the SAT? What is it used for?

Juniors and seniors in high school are the ones most likely to take the SAT. College admissions personnel use your test results as a way to decide if you can be accepted to their school. Because high schools across the nation have a variety of grading systems, the SAT score is designed to put all students on an equal footing. Your SAT score, along with your grades and other school information, helps colleges predict how well you will do at the college level.

If you score poorly on the SAT, it does not mean you should change your plans about going to college. Nor does it mean you will not do well in college. It just means you scored low. Should this happen, remember that you have options:

First, you can register to take the SAT again. Use the time before the next SAT administration to prepare as best you can.

Second, a poor score does not automatically shut the door to all colleges. College admissions officers use several criteria when reviewing applicants including your high school grades, your extracurricular activities, and the levels of your courses in high school.

Who administers the test?

ETS, a client of the College Board, which owns the SAT, develops and scores the test and currently administers it with the assistance of educators across the United States.

When is it best to take the SAT?

You should take the test as a junior or senior in high school. We recommend taking the SAT early in the school year. This allows you more time to retake the test if you are not satisfied with your first set of scores.

When and where do I take the SAT?

The SAT is normally offered seven times a year nationwide. The test can be taken at hundreds of locations throughout the country, including high schools. The standard test day is normally on Saturday, but alternate days are permitted if a conflict—such as a religious obligation—exists.

For information on upcoming SAT testing dates, see your guidance counselor for an SAT Registration Bulletin or request a registration bulletin from ETS as follows:

College Board SAT Program
PO Box 025505
Miami, FL 33102
Phone: (866) 756-7346
Contact Webpage: *www.collegeboard.com/inquiry/sathome.html*.

What about the registration fee?

You must pay a fee to register for the SAT. Some students may qualify to have this fee waived. To find out if you qualify for a fee waiver, contact your guidance counselor.

What is the Student Search Service?

The Student Search Service provides your SAT scores to colleges. Colleges enrolled in this service receive information about you, especially if you express interest in their school. On your SAT answer sheet, you can indicate that you want enrollment in this service.

PROVEN TEST-TAKING TIPS & STRATEGIES

There are many ways to familiarize yourself with the format of the SAT. Familiarization is a great way to help alleviate test day anxieties. The following list has ways to help you become accustomed to the SAT.

Become comfortable with the SAT's format: When practicing, simulate the conditions of the actual test. Pace yourself. Stay calm. After repeating this process a few times, you are boosting your chances of performing well on test day. Success breeds confidence, and your successes here will give you much more confidence on test day.

Read all of the possible answers: If you believe you know the correct answer to a question, it is best not to assume that your answer is automatically the correct answer. Read through all answer choices to ensure that you are not making an error by jumping to conclusions.

Use the process of elimination: Examine each answer to a question. Eliminate as many of the answer choices as possible. By eliminating just two answer choices, you have given yourself a better chance of the getting the correct answer out of the remaining three answer choices. Guess only if you can eliminate at least two answers. Remember that wrong answers are always penalized.

You don't have to answer every question: You are not penalized for not answering every question. Questions left blank are not counted. Maximize this advantage by using a smart guessing strategy to questions where you are unsure of the right answer. Always keep in mind that if you are truly stumped, you do not have to answer, especially because ¼ point is deducted for every wrong answer on multiple-choice questions.

Work quickly and steadily: You will only have 20 to 30 minutes to work on each section. Working quickly and steadily helps you avoid focusing too much attention and time on any one problem. Use the practice exams in this book to help you manage your timing.

Learn the directions and format for each section of the test: Familiarize yourself with the directions and format of each of the different test sections. This will help you avoid "direction shock" later on during the test, when you might read directions that were better read at the start of the test. Shocks like these cause nervousness. Nervousness causes mistakes. And these kinds of mistakes are completely avoidable.

Work on the easier questions first: The questions for each section of the SAT are arranged in ascending order of difficulty. The easier questions are at the beginning of each section, while the more difficult ones are at the end of the section. If you find yourself working too long on a single question, make a mark next to it in the test booklet and continue with the next question. After you have answered the remaining questions, return to the ones you skipped.

Mark answers carefully: Be sure that the answer sheet oval corresponds to the question and answer of your test booklet. Because the multiple-choice sections are graded mechanically, marking one wrong answer in this way can throw off your answer key and thus ruin your score. Be extremely careful.

Eliminating obviously wrong answers: Sometimes an SAT question has one or two answer choices that appear odd or out of place. These answers may be obviously wrong for one or more reasons:

- Impossible to achieve given the problem's conditions
- Violation of mathematical rules or principles
- Simply illogical

Being able to spot obviously wrong answers before you finish a problem gives you an advantage because you are able to make a better educated guess from the remaining choices. This works best when you find yourself unable to fully solve a problem.

Working from answer choices: Turn the multiple-choice format to your advantage by working backwards from the answer choices to solve a problem. This strategy is not applicable to all questions, but it is helpful when you can plug choices into a given formula or equation. The answer choices often narrow the scope of responses allowing you to make an educated guess based on eliminating choices that you know do not fit the problem.

AFTER THE TEST

Once your test materials have been collected, you will be dismissed. Then your day is free. Go home and relax. Or reward yourself with some shopping. Or play a video game. Or hang with friends. The good news is that the hard part is over. Now you just have to wait for the results.

PART I

MULTIPLE-CHOICE QUESTIONS

The Multiple-Choice questions of the SAT's math section are designed to test your ability to solve problems involving arithmetic, algebra, geometry, and data analysis. A few of the problems may be similar to those found in a math textbook and will require nothing more than the use of basic rules and formulas. Most of the problems, however, will require more than that. Multiple-Choice questions will ask you to think creatively and apply basic skills to solve problems.

All Multiple-Choice questions are in a format with five possible responses. There are a number of advantages and disadvantages associated with multiple-choice math tests. Learning what some of these advantages and disadvantages are can help you improve your test performance.

The greatest disadvantage of a multiple-choice math test is that every question presents you with four wrong answers. These wrong answers are not randomly chosen numbers—they are the answers that students are most likely to get if they make certain mistakes. They also tend to be answers that "look right" to someone who does not know how to solve the problem. Thus, on a particular problem, you may be relieved to find "your" answer among the answer choices, only to discover later that you fell into a common error trap. Wrong answer choices can also distract or confuse you when you are attempting to solve a problem correctly, causing you to question your answer even though it is right.

The greatest *advantage* of a multiple-choice math test is that the right answer is also presented to you. This means that you may be able to spot the right answer even if you do not understand a problem completely or do not have time to finish it. It means that you may be able to pick the right answer by guessing intelligently. It also means that you may be saved from getting a problem wrong when the answer you obtain is not among the answer choices—and you have to go back and work the problem again.

Keep in mind, also, that the use of a calculator is permitted during the test. Do not be tempted, however, to use this as a crutch. Some problems can actually be solved more quickly without a calculator, and you still have to work through the problem to know what numbers to punch. No calculator in the world can solve a problem for you.

ABOUT THE DIRECTIONS

The directions found at the beginning of each Multiple-Choice section are simple—solve each problem, then mark the best of five answer choices on your answer sheet. Following these instructions, however, is important information that you should understand thoroughly before you attempt to take a test. This information includes definitions of standard symbols and formulas that you may need to solve Multiple-Choice problems. The formulas are given so that you don't have to memorize them—however, to benefit from this information, you need to know what is and what is not included. Otherwise, you may waste time looking for a formula that is not listed, or you may fail to look for a formula that is listed. The formulas given to you at the beginning of a Multiple-Choice section include:

- The number of degrees in a straight line

- Area and circumference of a circle; number of degrees in a circle; volume of a cylinder

- Area of a triangle; Pythagorean Theorem for a right triangle; sum of angle measures of a triangle; the length of the sides of a 45-45-90 triangle and a 30-60-90 triangle.

- Area of a rectangle; volume of a rectangular solid

Following the formulas and definitions of symbols is a very important statement about the diagrams, or figures, that may accompany Multiple-Choice questions. This statement tells you that, unless stated otherwise in a specific question, figures are drawn to scale.

ABOUT THE QUESTIONS

Most Multiple-Choice math questions on the SAT fall into one of four categories: numbers and operations; algebra and functions; geometry and measurement; and data analysis, statistics, and probability. In the following sections, we will review the kinds of questions you will encounter on the actual test.

NUMBER AND OPERATION QUESTIONS

Most number and operation questions on the SAT fall into one of the following three question types. For each question type, an example and solution will be given, highlighting strategies and techniques for completing the problems as quickly as possible.

Question Type 1: Evaluating Expressions

Number and operation questions on the SAT often ask you to find the value of an arithmetic expression or to find the value of a missing term in an expression. The temptation when you see one of these expressions is to calculate its value—a process that is time-consuming and can easily lead to an error. A better way to approach an arithmetic expression is to use your knowledge of properties of numbers to spot shortcuts.

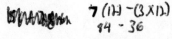

PROBLEM

$7(8 + 4) - (3 \times 12) =$

(A) 24

(B) 48

(C) 110

(D) 144

(E) 3,024

SOLUTION

Before you jump into multiplication, look at the numbers inside the first parentheses. This is the sum $(8 + 4) = 12$, which makes the entire expression equal to $7(12) - (3 \times 12)$. The distributive property tells you that $a(b + c) = ab + ac$ and $a(b - c) = ab - ac$. The expression $7(12) - (3 \times 12)$ can be made to fit the second formula, with a equal to 12, and 7 and 3 equal to b and c, respectively. Thus, $7(12) - (3 \times 12)$ becomes $12(7 - 3)$, and the answer is simply 12×4, or 48.

Question Type 2: Undefined Symbols

Most SAT math sections include problems that involve undefined symbols. In some problems, these symbols define a value by asking you to perform several arithmetic operations. For example, the symbol $\boxed{x}$ may tell you to square some number x then subtract 3: $\boxed{x} = x^2 - 3$. In other problems, a symbol may represent a missing numeral, such as $10 - \Delta = 7$. By looking at the arithmetic, you can see that Δ must equal 3.

PROBLEM

Let $[n] = n^2 + 1$ for all numbers n. Which of the following is equal to the product of $[2]$ and $[3]$?

(A) $[6]$ (D) $[9]$

(B) $[7]$ (E) $[11]$

(C) $[8]$

SOLUTION

The newly defined symbol is $[\ ]$. To find the values for $[2]$ and $[3]$, plug them into the formula $[n] = n^2 + 1$.

$[2] = 2^2 + 1 = 4 + 1 = 5$

$[3] = 3^2 + 1 = 9 + 1 = 10$

Since $[2] = 5$, and $[3] = 10$, we can compute the product: $5 \times 10 = 50$.

Now look at the answers. You will see that the answers are given in terms of $[\ ]$. Once again, you must plug them into the formula $[n] = n^2 + 1$. If we plug each answer choice into the equation, we get

$[6] = 6^2 + 1 = 36 + 1 = 37$

$[7] = 7^2 + 1 = 49 + 1 = 50$

$[8] = 8^2 + 1 = 64 + 1 = 65$

$[9] = 9^2 + 1 = 81 + 1 = 82$

$[11] = 11^2 + 1 = 121 + 1 = 122$

Question Type 3: Sets

A **set** is a group of items. Each item in a set is called an **element** of that set. For example, let set X represent the set of positive odd integers between 0 and 10. This set has five elements: the numbers 1, 3, 5, 7, and 9. The elements of a set are often written within brackets, as shown next.

$X = \{1, 3, 5, 7, 9\}$

The **union** of two sets includes all of the elements in the first set and all of the elements in the second set. If set $Y = \{6, 7, 8, 9\}$, then the union of sets X and Y is the set $\{1, 3, 5, 6, 7, 8, 9\}$.

The **intersection** of two sets includes only the elements that the two sets have in common. The intersection of sets X and Y is the set $\{7, 9\}$.

One way to show the relationship between two sets is with a Venn diagram. In a Venn diagram, each set is represented by a circle. The intersection of the sets is represented by the area where the circles overlap. The following Venn diagram shows sets x and y. The shaded area shows their intersection.

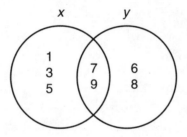

PROBLEM

The set M includes all the integers greater than 12 and less than 24, set N includes all the even integers greater than 4 and less than 20, and set P includes all even integers greater than 8 and less than 28 the sum of whose digits is less than 5.
Which set is equal to $M \cap N \cap P$?

(A) $\{14, 16\}$ (D) $\{14\}$

(B) $\{16, 18\}$ (E) $M \cap N \cap P$ is an empty set

(C) $\{18\}$

SOLUTION

(E)   We are given $M = \{13, 14, 15, 16, 17, 18, 19, 20, 21, 22, 23\}$, $N = \{6, 8, 10, 12, 14, 16, 18\}$, and $P = \{10, 12, 20, 22\}$. We have $M \cap P = \{14, 16, 18\}$. Therefore, $M \cap N \cap P = \varnothing$ (that is, an empty set).

ALGEBRA AND FUNCTION QUESTIONS

Algebra and function problems use letters or variables to represent numbers. In these types of problems, you will be required to solve existing algebraic expressions or translate word problems into algebraic expressions.

Question Type 1: Algebraic Expressions

Problems involving algebraic expressions often contain hidden shortcuts. You can find these shortcuts by asking yourself, "How can this expression be rearranged?" Often rearrangement will cause an answer to appear almost magically.

There are three basic ways in which you can rearrange an algebraic expression. You can

1. **combine like terms.**

2. **factor the expression.**

3. **multiply out the expression.**

PROBLEM

If $x = \frac{1}{2}$, which of the following equals $x^2 - x + \frac{1}{4}$?

(A) $-\dfrac{1}{2}$ (D) $\dfrac{1}{2}$

(B) 0   (E) 1

(C) $\dfrac{1}{4}$

SOLUTION

You can find the answer by substituting $x = \frac{1}{2}$ into the given expression, but there is an easier way. Look at $x^2 - x + \frac{1}{4}$. Remembering the strategy tip, this expression is equal to the trinomial square $(x - \frac{1}{2})^2$. Now you can see at a glance that since you are told that

$$x = \tfrac{1}{2}, \ (x - \tfrac{1}{2})^2$$

must equal 0. Thus, the answer is (B).

Question Type 2: Word Problems

Among the most common types of word problems found on the SAT are age problems, mixture problems, distance problems, and percent problems. There is a strategy, however, that can help you to solve all types of word problems— learning to recognize "keywords."

Keywords are words or phrases that can be translated directly into a mathematical symbol, expression, or operation. As you know, you usually cannot solve a word problem without writing some kind of equation. Learning to spot keywords will enable you to write the equations you need more easily.

Listed below are some of the most common keywords. As you practice solving word problems, you will probably find others.

Keyword	Mathematical Equivalent
is	equals
sum	add
plus	add
more than, older than	add
difference	subtract
less than, younger than	subtract
twice, double	multiply by 2
half as many	divided by 2
increase by 3	add 3
decrease by 3	subtract 3

PROBLEM

Adam has 50 more than twice the number of "frequent flier" miles that Erica has. If Adam has 200 frequent flier miles, how many does Erica have?

(A) 25

(B) 60

(C) 75

(D) 100

(E) 250

SOLUTION

The keywords in this problem are "more" and "twice." If you let a = the number of frequent flier miles that Adam has and e = the number of frequent flier miles that Erica has, you can write: $a = 50 + 2e$. Since $a = 200$, the solution becomes: $200 = 50 + 2e$. Therefore, $200 - 50 = 2e$, or $150 = 2e$, and $\frac{150}{2} = e$ or $75 = e$, which is choice (C).

Question Type 3: Functions as Models

Some questions on the SAT will involve functions that model real-world situations. In some cases, you may be asked to apply a given function rule to solve a problem. In others, you may be asked to select a graph or an equation that models a given set of data.

Once you have identified a function that seems to model a situation, it is important to check that the function gives the correct output values for all available input values.

PROBLEM

Cost of Sleeping Bag Rental				
Number of Days (x)	2	4	6	8
Cost (y)	$17	$27	$37	$47

The table shows a linear relationship between the cost of renting a sleeping bag and the number of days the sleeping bag is rented. Which of the following models the rental cost y as a function of the number of days x?

(A) $y = x + 15$ (D) $y = 6x + 5$

(B) $y = 2x + 10$ (E) $y = 9x - 1$

(C) $y = 5x + 7$

SOLUTION

The pattern in the table shows that every increase of 2 days results in an increase of $10 in cost. Therefore, the slope of the linear function that models this relationship is $\frac{10}{2}$, or 5. The only answer choice with a slope of 5 is choice (C), $y = 5x + 7$. You can check that this equation is correct by mentally substituting each x-value from the table and verifying that the equation produces the correct set of y-values.

Notice that choices (A), (D), and (E) each give the correct y-value when $x = 2$. These choices are incorrect, however, because they fail to produce the correct y-values when x equals 4, 6, or 8.

GEOMETRY AND MEASUREMENT QUESTIONS

SAT geometry and measurement questions require you to find the area or missing sides of figures given certain information. These problems require you to use "if . . . then" reasoning or to draw figures based on given information.

Question Type 1: "If . . . Then" Reasoning

You will not have to work with geometric proofs on the SAT, but the logic used in proofs can help you enormously when it comes to solving SAT geometry problems. This type of logic is often referred to as "if . . . then" reasoning. In "if . . . then" reasoning, you say to yourself, "If A is true, then B must be true." By using "if . . . then" reasoning, you can draw conclusions based on the rules and definitions that you know. For example, you might say, "If ABC is a triangle, then the sum of its angles must equal 180°."

PROBLEM

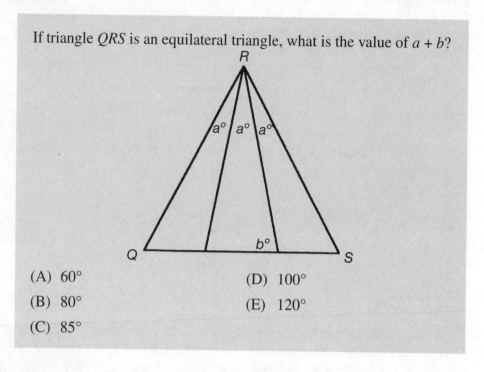

If triangle QRS is an equilateral triangle, what is the value of $a + b$?

(A) 60°

(B) 80°

(C) 85°

(D) 100°

(E) 120°

SOLUTION

You can obtain the information that you need to solve this problem by using a series of "if . . . then" statements: "If QRS is an equilateral triangle, then each angle must equal 60°." "If angle $R = 60°$, then a must equal 20°." "If $a = 20°$, then b must equal half of $(180° − 20°)$ or 80°." "If $a = 20°$ and $b = 80°$, then $a + b = 100°$." Therefore, answer (D) is correct.

Question Type 2: Drawing Diagrams

Among the most difficult geometry problems on the SAT are those that describe a geometric situation without providing a diagram. For these problems, you must learn to draw your own diagram based on the information that is given. The best way to do this is step-by-step, using each piece of information that the problem provides. As you draw, you should always remember to:

1. label all points, angles, and line segments according to the information provided.

2. indicate parallel or perpendicular lines.

3. write in any measures that you are given.

PROBLEM

If vertical line segment $\overline{AB}$ is perpendicular to line segment $\overline{CD}$ at point O and if ray OE bisects angle BOD, what is the value of angle AOE?

(A) 45°   (D) 135°

(B) 90°   (E) 180°

(C) 120°

SOLUTION

Draw as follows:

Draw and label vertical line segment $\overline{AB}$.

Draw and label line segment $\overline{CD}$ perpendicular to $\overline{AB}$. Label the right angle that is formed. Label point O.

Locate angle BOD. Draw and label ray OE so that it bisects, or cuts into two equal parts, angle BOD. Use equal marks to show that the two parts of the angle are equal. Since you are bisecting a right angle, you can write in the measure 45°.

   Your diagram should resemble that shown below. Now you can evaluate your drawing to answer the question. Angle AOE is equal to 90° + 45°, or 135°. The answer is (D).

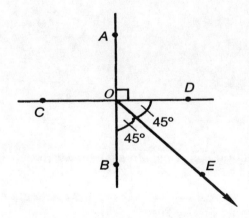

Question Type 3: Behavior of Graphs of Functions

A new type of question on the SAT will involve graphs of functions that are neither linear nor quadratic. You will be presented with a graph of such a function
and asked to draw a conclusion about it.

To answer these types of questions, you do not need to know how to write
the equation of the graphed function, but you will need to be able to identify the
coordinates of points that lie on the function's graph.

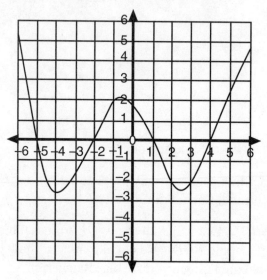

PROBLEM

A function *f* is graphed as shown. Based on this graph, for what values of *x* is the value of *f(x)* negative?

(A) $x < -5$ and $x > 4$ (D) $-4 < x < -3$ and $-2 < x < 3$

(B) $x < -2$ and $x > 1$ (E) $-5 < x < -2$ and $1 < x < 4$

(C) $-2 < x < 1$

SOLUTION

The value of the function $f(x)$ is negative whenever the y-value of the graph of
the function is negative. The y-values are negative for sections of the graph of
the function that lie below the x-axis. There are two sections of the function's
graph that lie below the x-axis. The first section occurs when the x-values are
between –5 and –2. The second section occurs when the x-values are between 1

and 4. Therefore, the value of $f(x)$ is negative when $-5 < x < -2$ and when $1 < x < 4$, making choice (E) the correct answer.

DATA ANALYSIS, STATISTICS, AND PROBABILITY QUESTIONS

Question Type 1: Data Interpretation

Data interpretation problems usually require two basic steps. First, you have to read a chart or graph to obtain certain information. Then you have to apply or manipulate the information to obtain an answer.

PROBLEM

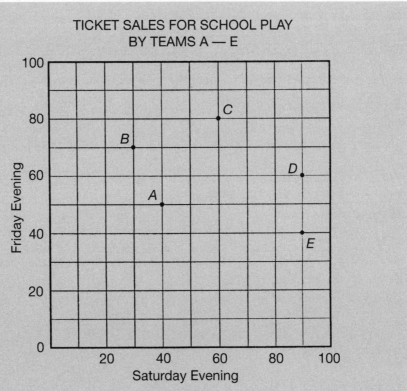

TICKET SALES FOR SCHOOL PLAY
BY TEAMS A — E

Which team sold the greatest number of tickets for Friday evening and Saturday evening combined?

(A) Team A   (D) Team D

(B) Team B   (E) Team E

(C) Team C

SOLUTION

Glancing over the data, you see that the number of tickets sold for Friday evening is represented vertically, while the number of tickets sold for Saturday evening is represented horizontally. Points placed on the grid represent each team's ticket sales for the two evenings.

Read the graph to determine the number of tickets sold by each team for Friday evening and Saturday evening.

Add each pair of numbers to find the total number of tickets sold by each team for both evenings.

Compare the totals to see which team sold the most tickets.

The answer is (D), since team D sold 60 tickets for Friday evening and 90 tickets for Saturday evening for a highest total of 150.

Question Type 2: Mean, Median, and Mode

All three of these numbers are measures of central tendency. They describe the "middle" or "center" of the data.

The mean is the arithmetic average. It is the sum of the variables divided by the total number of variables. For example, the mean of 4, 3, and 8 is

$$\frac{4+3+8}{3} = \frac{15}{3} = 5.$$

PROBLEM

Find the mean salary for four company employees who make $5/hr., $8/hr., $12/hr., and $15/hr.

(A) $5/hr   (D) $20/hr.

(B) $10/hr.   (E) $8/hr.

(C) $15/hr.

SOLUTION

The mean salary is the average.

$$\frac{\$5 + \$8 + \$12 + \$15}{4} = \frac{\$40}{10} = \$10 / hr.$$

The correct answer is (B).

The median is the middle value in a set when there is an odd number of values. There is an equal number of values larger and smaller than the median. When the set is an even number of values, the average of the two middle values is the median. For example:

The median of (2, 3, 5, 8, 9) is 5.

The median of (2, 3, 5, 9, 10, 11) is $\dfrac{5+9}{2} = 7$.

PROBLEM

For this series of observations find the median.
500, 600, 800, 800, 900, 900, 900, 900, 900, 1,000, 1,100

(A) 500   (D) 900

(B) 600   (E) 1,000

(C) 800

SOLUTION

The median is the value appearing in the middle. We have 11 values, so here the sixth, 900, is the median. The correct answer is (D).

PROBLEM

Nine rats run through a maze. The time in minutes each rat took to traverse the maze is recorded and these times (in minutes) are listed below.

1.0, 2.5, 3, 1.5, 2, 1.25, 1.0, 0.9, 30

For this series find the mode.

(A) 1.0   (D) 0.9

(B) 2.5   (E) 30

(C) 1.25

SOLUTION

The mode is the most frequently occurring value in the sample. In this data set the mode is 1.0. The correct answer is (A).

Question Type 3: Scatterplots

A **scatterplot** shows the relationship between two sets of data. Some word problems may ask you to interpret the data in a scatterplot or draw conclusions about its line of best fit.

PROBLEM

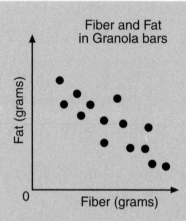

The scatterplot shows the relationship between the grams of fiber and the grams of fat in several brands of granola. Describe the slope of the line of best fit for the data in this scatterplot.

(A) As *x* decreases, *y* decreases

(B) As *x* increases, *y* increases

(C) As *x* increases, *y* increases then decreases

(D) As *x* increases, *y* decreases

(E) *y* varies neither directly nor inversely as *x*

SOLUTION

The data in the scatterplot show a trend. As the number of grams of fiber in the granola increases, the number of grams of fat tends to decrease. The line of best fit for the data moves downward as it moves from left to right. Therefore, the slope of the line of best fit is negative. The correct choice is (D).

Question Type 4: Geometric Probability

These types of problems involve the probability of events that are related to geometric figures. For example, a problem may involve finding the probability that a randomly selected point will lie in a specific area within a larger geometric figure.

PROBLEM

The circular target below has a radius of 12 in. The inner circle of the target has a radius of 6 in. If an arrow strikes the target at a random point, what is the probability that the arrow will strike the shaded region?

(A) $\dfrac{1}{2}$ (D) $\dfrac{7}{9}$

(B) $\dfrac{3}{4}$ (E) $\dfrac{4}{5}$

(C) $\dfrac{4}{3}$

SOLUTION

The probability that the arrow will strike the shaded region is the ratio of the area of the shaded region to the area of the entire target. First, find the area of the entire target, which has a radius of 12 in.

$$\text{Area of entire target: } A = \pi r^2 = \pi(12)^2 = 144\pi \text{ in.}^2$$

The area of the shaded region is equal to the area of the entire target minus the area of the inner circle.

$$\text{Area of inner circle: } A = \pi r^2 = \pi(6)^2 = 36\pi \text{ in.}^2$$

$$\text{Area of shaded region: } 144\pi - 36\pi = 108\pi \text{ in.}^2$$

The probability that the arrow will strike the shaded region is equal to the ratio $\frac{180\pi}{144\pi}$, which simplifies to $\frac{3}{4}$. The answer is (B).

ANSWERING MULTIPLE-CHOICE QUESTIONS

The following steps should be used to help guide you through answering Multiple-Choice questions. Combined with the review material you have just studied, these steps will provide you with the tools necessary to answer correctly the questions you will encounter.

STEP 1   Try to determine the type of question with which you are dealing. This will help you focus in on how to attack the question.

STEP 2   Carefully read all of the information presented. Make sure you are answering the question, and not incorrectly reading the question. Look for keywords that can help you determine what the question is asking.

STEP 3   Perform the operations indicated, but be sure you are taking the easiest approach. Simplify all expressions and equations before performing your calculations. Draw your own figures if a question refers to them, but does not provide them.

STEP 4   Try to work backwards from the answer choices if you are having difficulty determining an answer.

STEP 5   If you are still having difficulty determining an answer, use the process of elimination. If you can eliminate at least two choices, you will greatly increase your chances of correctly answering the question. Eliminating three choices means that you have a fifty-fifty chance of correctly answering the question if you guess.

STEP 6   Once you have chosen an answer, fill in the oval which corresponds to the question and answer which you have chosen. Beware of stray lines on your answer sheet, as they may cause your answers to be scored incorrectly.

Now, use the information you have just learned to answer the following questions.

DRILLS

DIRECTIONS: Solve each problem, using any available space on the page for scratch work. Then decide which answer choice is the best and fill in the corresponding oval on the answer sheet.

NOTES

(1) The use of a calculator is permitted. All numbers used are real numbers.

(2) Figures that accompany problems in this test are intended to provide information useful in solving the problems. They are drawn as accurately as possible EXCEPT when it is stated in a specific problem that the figure is not drawn to scale. All figures lie in a plane unless otherwise indicated.

REFERENCE INFORMATION

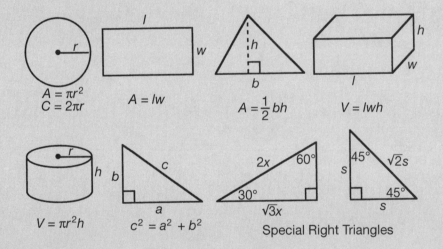

$$A = \pi r^2$$
$$C = 2\pi r$$

$$A = lw$$

$$A = \frac{1}{2}bh$$

$$V = lwh$$

$$V = \pi r^2 h$$

$$c^2 = a^2 + b^2$$

Special Right Triangles

The number of degrees of arc in a circle is 360.

The measure in degrees of a straight angle is 180.

The sum of the measures in degrees of the angles of a triangle is 180.

■ PROBLEM I.1

If $f(x) = 3x^2 - x + 5$, then $f(3) =$

(A) 15.   (D) 27.

(B) 17.   (E) 29.

(C) 23.

SOLUTION

(E)   You are given the function $f(x) = 3x^2 - x + 5$.

To find $f(3)$ means to find out what the given function equals when you let x equal 3. Thus, $f(3)$ is found by substituting 3 in place of x, everywhere that x appears

$$f(3) = 3x^2 - x + 5$$

$$f(3) = 3 \times 3^2 - 3 + 5$$

$$= 3 \times 9 - 3 + 5$$

$$= 27 - 3 + 5$$

$$= 24 + 5$$

$$= 29$$

So, the correct answer is (E).

Note: $f(x)$ is pronounced "f of x," and

$f(3)$ is pronounced "f of 3."

■ PROBLEM I.2

A runner takes 9 seconds to run a distance of 132 feet. What is the runner's speed in miles per hour?

(A) 9   (D) 12

(B) 10   (E) 13

(C) 11

SOLUTION

(B) The runner's speed is $\dfrac{132 \text{ feet}}{9 \text{ sec.}}$.

Speed is always a distance (in this case "feet") divided by a time (in this case "seconds"). Note, though, that the problem asks for speed in miles per hour, *not* in feet per second. Thus, the rest of the problem consists of converting to the desired miles per hour.

Here's our plan:

Step I—Convert the numerator from feet to miles.

Step II—Convert the denominator from seconds to hours.

Step III—Divide the new numerator by the new denominator. (Remember that "per" indicates division, so miles per hour means miles/hour).

Step I

(a) Recall that 5,280 feet = 1 mile.

(b) Multiply (132 feet) by the conversion factor $\left(\dfrac{1 \text{ mile}}{5{,}280 \text{ feet}}\right)$.

$$(132 \text{ feet}) \times \left(\frac{1 \text{ mile}}{5{,}280 \text{ feet}}\right) = \frac{132}{5{,}280} \text{ mile}$$

$$= .025 \text{ mile}$$

(c) Notice that we cancelled the word "feet" in the numerator with the word "feet" in the denominator, *just as if they were numbers*. This left us with "miles" in the numerator, which is what we wanted.

(d) In step (b) above, we were careful to choose the conversion factor

$$\left(\frac{1 \text{ mile}}{5{,}280 \text{ feet}}\right)$$

rather than the other possibility

$$\left(\frac{5{,}280 \text{ feet}}{1 \text{ mile}}\right),$$

so "feet" would cancel.

Step II

Next, we convert (9 sec.) to hours.

(a)   Recall that 1 hour = 60 min., and 1 min. = 60 sec.

(b)   Multiply (9 sec.) by two conversion factors.

$$(9 \text{ sec.}) \times \left(\frac{1 \text{ min.}}{60 \text{ sec.}}\right) \times \left(\frac{1 \text{ hour}}{60 \text{ min.}}\right) = \frac{9}{60 \times 60} \text{ hour}$$

$$= \frac{9}{3,600} \text{ hour}$$

$$= \frac{1}{400} \text{ hour}$$

$$= .0025 \text{ hour}$$

Step III

Combining the results from Step I and Step II gives

$$\left(\frac{132 \text{ feet}}{9 \text{ sec.}}\right) = \frac{.025 \text{ mile}}{.0025 \text{ hour}} = 10 \text{ miles/hour.}$$

So, the correct answer is (B).

Note: The entire problem can be done in one step, but you should only do this if you feel able to keep track of all the factors.

$$\left(\frac{132 \text{ feet}}{9 \text{ sec.}}\right) \left(\frac{1 \text{ mile}}{5,280 \text{ feet}}\right) \left(\frac{60 \text{ sec.}}{1 \text{ min.}}\right) \left(\frac{60 \text{ min}}{1 \text{ hour}}\right)$$

$$= \frac{132 \times 60 \times 60}{9 \times 5,280} \text{ miles/hour}$$

$$= 10 \text{ miles/hour}$$

■ PROBLEM I.3

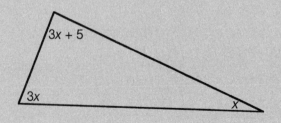

For the triangle pictured below, the degree measure of the three angles are x, $3x$, and $3x + 5$. Find x.

(A) 25

(B) 27

(C) 28

(D) 28.3

(E) 29

SOLUTION

(A)   Every triangle has three angles inside.

When you add together the measures of these three angles, you will always get 180°, no matter what size or shape the triangle is.

first angle + second angle + third angle = 180

$$x + 3x + (3x + 5) = 180$$

Group like terms together (terms containing an x).

$$(x + 3x + 3x) + 5 = 180$$

Add like terms.

$$7x + 5 = 180$$

Subtract 5 from both sides.

$$7x + 5 - 5 = 180 - 5$$
$$7x = 175$$

Divide both sides by 7.

$$\frac{7x}{7} = \frac{175}{7}$$
$$x = 25$$

So, the correct answer is (A).

■ PROBLEM I.4

Divide $3\frac{1}{5}$ by $1\frac{1}{3}$.

(A) $2\frac{2}{5}$

(D) $4\frac{4}{15}$

(B) $3\frac{1}{15}$

(E) 8

(C) $3\frac{3}{5}$

SOLUTION

(A)   We are asked to find $\dfrac{3\frac{1}{5}}{1\frac{1}{3}}$.

To do this, we must first change both mixed numbers into improper fractions.

$$3\frac{1}{5} = \frac{(3\times 5)+1}{5} = \frac{15+1}{5} = \frac{16}{5}$$

$$1\frac{1}{3} = \frac{(1\times 3)+1}{3} = \frac{3+1}{3} = \frac{4}{3}$$

So, $\dfrac{3\frac{1}{5}}{1\frac{1}{3}} = \dfrac{\frac{16}{5}}{\frac{4}{3}}$.

Observe that $\dfrac{\frac{16}{5}}{\frac{4}{3}}$ is in the form $\dfrac{\frac{a}{b}}{\frac{c}{d}}$.

Also, recall that $\dfrac{\frac{a}{b}}{\frac{c}{d}} = \dfrac{a}{b} \times \dfrac{d}{c}$.

Thus, $\dfrac{\frac{16}{5}}{\frac{4}{3}} = \dfrac{16}{5} \times \dfrac{3}{4}$

$$= \frac{16 \times 3}{5 \times 4}$$

$$= \frac{4 \times 4 \times 3}{5 \times 4}$$

(Wrote 16 as 4 × 4)

$$= \frac{12}{5}$$

(Cancelled 4 from the numerator and denominator)

The final step is to change $\frac{12}{5}$ (an improper fraction) into a mixed number by dividing the denominator, 5, into the numerator, 12.

$$\frac{12}{5} = 2 + \frac{2}{5} = 2\frac{2}{5}$$

So, the correct answer is (A).

◼ PROBLEM I.5

Change 125.937% to a decimal.

(A) 1.25937
(B) 12.5937
(C) 125.937

(D) 1,259.37
(E) 12,593.7

SOLUTION

(A)   To change a percent to a decimal, drop the percent sign and move the decimal point two place values to the left.

You can see why this is true:

$$125.937\% = \frac{125.937}{100}$$

(Definition of percent)

$$= 1.25937$$

(Division by 100 moves decimal point two places to the left)

So, the correct choice is (A).

◼ PROBLEM I.6

Evaluate $4(a + b) + 2[5 - (a^2 + b^2)]$, if $a = 2$ and $b = 1$.

(A) 6
(B) 7
(C) 12

(D) 20
(E) 62

SOLUTION

(C)   Every place you see an a, substitute 2.

Every place you see a b, substitute 1.

Remember to:

Simplify quantities inside parentheses first.

Simplify inner parentheses before outer parentheses.

$4 (a + b) + 2 [5 - (a^2 + b^2)]$ (Given)

$= 4 (2 + 1) + 2 [5 - (2^2 + 1^2)]$ (Substituted for a and b)

$= 4 (3) + 2 [5 - (4 + 1)]$

$= 12 + 2 [5 - (5)]$

$= 12 + 2 [0]$

$= 12 + 0$

$= 12$

So, the correct choice is (C).

■ PROBLEM I.7

Find the mean of the following scores:
     5, 7, 9, 8, 5, 8, 9, 8, 7, 8, 7, 5, 9, 5, 8, 5, 9, 6, 5

(A) 5   (D) 8

(B) 6   (E) 9

(C) 7

SOLUTION

(C)   We need to apply the definition of the mean to our problem.

$$\text{Mean} = \frac{\text{sum of the scores}}{\text{how many scores there are}}$$

Sum of the scores (add them)

$$= 5 + 7 + 9 + 8 + 5 + 8 + 9 + 8 + 7 + 8 + 7 + 5 + 9$$
$$+ 5 + 8 + 5 + 9 + 6 + 5$$

$$= 133$$

Number of scores (count them) $= 19$

Thus, mean $= \frac{133}{19} = 7$

The correct answer is (C).

PROBLEM I.8

What percent of 260 is 13?

(A) .05% (D) .5%

(B) 5% (E) 20%

(C) 50%

SOLUTION

(B) We must translate certain keywords from the given word problem into their mathematical equivalents, as follows:

"of" translates to × (multiplication)

"is" translates to = (equals)

"what percent" translates to x (the unknown in decimal form)

Now we can re-write the question as an equation.

(What percent) (of) 260 (is) 13

$x \times 260 = 13$

or, $260x = 13$

$$x = \frac{13}{260} = .05 = \frac{05}{100} = 5\%$$

So, the answer should be (B).

PROBLEM I.9

How many corners does a cube have?

(A) 4 (D) 12

(B) 6 (E) 24

(C) 8

SOLUTION

(C)   Referring to the figure, we see that the cube has *eight* corners.

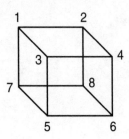

The top has four corners (points 1, 2, 3, and 4).

The bottom has four corners (points 5, 6, 7, and 8).

So, the correct choice is (C).

■ PROBLEM I.10

Subtract $4\frac{1}{3} - 1\frac{5}{6}$.

(A) $3\frac{2}{3}$ (D) $2\frac{1}{6}$

(B) $2\frac{1}{2}$ (E) $3\frac{1}{6}$

(C) $3\frac{1}{2}$

SOLUTION

(B)   Subtract $4\frac{1}{3} - 1\frac{5}{6}$.

Change the given numbers to improper fractions.

$$4\frac{1}{3} - 1\frac{5}{6} = \frac{(4 \times 3) + 1}{3} - \frac{(1 \times 6) + 5}{6}$$

$$= \frac{13}{3} - \frac{11}{6}$$

$$= \left[\left(\frac{13}{3}\right)\left(\frac{2}{2}\right)\right] - \frac{11}{6} \qquad \text{(Common denominator is 6)}$$

$$= \frac{26}{6} - \frac{11}{6}$$

$$= \frac{26 - 11}{6}$$

$$= \frac{15}{6}$$

Change $\frac{15}{6}$ into a mixed number.

$$\frac{15}{6} = 2 + \frac{3}{6} = 2 + \frac{1}{2} = 2\frac{1}{2}$$

So, the correct answer is (B).

■ PROBLEM I.11

The rates of a laundry are $6.25 for the first 15 pieces and $0.35 for each additional piece. If the laundry charge is $8.35, how many pieces were laundered?

(A) 5

(B) 6

(C) 15

(D) 21

(E) 25

SOLUTION

(D)   The total laundry charge is $8.35.

Subtracting $6.25 (the cost of the first 15 pieces of laundry) gives:

$8.35 − $6.25 = $2.10.

We want to find how many additional pieces (beyond the first 15) were laundered for this remaining $2.10.

We can use a proportion.

$$\frac{\$.35}{1 \text{ piece}} = \frac{\$2.10}{x \text{ pieces}}$$

Cross multiplying gives

$$.35x = 2.10$$

$$x = \frac{2.10}{.35} = 6 \text{ additional pieces}$$

The total number of pieces is

15 (at a cost of $6.25) + 6 (at a cost of $2.10) = 21 pieces.

So, the choice should be (D).

◼ PROBLEM I.12

The enrollment in Eastern High School is 1,050. If the attendance on a certain day was 94%, how many students were absent that day?

(A) 50   (D) 987

(B) 63   (E) 1,044

(C) 420

SOLUTION

(B)   If 94% attended, then 6% did *not* attend (were absent). (This was found by subtracting 100% – 94% = 6%.)

Number absent = 6% of total enrollment

$$= 6\% \times 1,050$$

$$= .06 \times 1,050 \ (6\% \text{ in its decimal form, is } .06)$$

$$= 63$$

So, the correct answer is (B).

◼ PROBLEM I.13

Find the correct solution to the nearest cent: 15% of $8.75.

(A) $1.31   (D) $13.13

(B) $1.32   (E) $131.25

(C) $13.12

SOLUTION

(A)   15% of $8.75 = .15 \times \$8.75$

$$= \$1.3125$$

Since we are working with dollars and cents, we must round this number to two decimal places (the nearest penny). To do this, look at the digit to the right of the second decimal place. This digit is 2. 2 is less than 5, so we round $1.3125 down to $1.31. ($1.3125 is closer to $1.31 than it is to $1.32.)

So, the correct answer is (A).

■ PROBLEM I.14

Simplify $6\sqrt{7} + 4\sqrt{7} - \sqrt{5} + 5\sqrt{7}$.

(A) $10\sqrt{7}$ (D) $15\sqrt{16}$

(B) $15\sqrt{7} - \sqrt{5}$ (E) 60

(C) $15\sqrt{21} - \sqrt{5}$

SOLUTION

(B) $6\sqrt{7} + 4\sqrt{7} - \sqrt{5} + 5\sqrt{7}$

(Given)

$$= \left(6\sqrt{7} + 4\sqrt{7} + 5\sqrt{7}\right) - \sqrt{5}$$

(Grouped together terms containing $\sqrt{7}$)

$$= (6 + 4 + 5)\sqrt{7} - \sqrt{5}$$

(Factored out $\sqrt{7}$ from parentheses)

$$= 15\sqrt{7} - \sqrt{5}$$

(Added $6 + 4 + 5$ to get 15)

So, the correct answer is (B).

▪ PROBLEM I.15

$4\% \times 4\% =$

(A) 0.0016%   (D) 16%

(B) 0.16%   (E) 160%

(C) 1.6%

SOLUTION

(B) $4\% \times 4\% = .04 \times .04$ (Wrote % in decimal form)

$$= .0016$$

This is the answer in decimal form; notice, though, that your choices are given in % form. Thus, we need to change the decimal to a percent by moving the decimal point two places to the right and adding a percent sign.

$$.0016 = .16\%$$

So, the correct answer is (B).

▪ PROBLEM I.16

If $x - (4x - 8) + 9 + (6x - 8) = 9 - x + 24$, then $x =$

(A) 4.   (D) 6.

(B) 2.   (E) 10.

(C) 8.

SOLUTION

(D)   The goal is to get x alone on the left side.

$x - (4x - 8) + 9 + (6x - 8) = 9 - x + 24$ (Given)

Distribute minus sign into the first set of parentheses. Note that this gives a *positive* 8.

$x - 4x + 8 + 9 + (6x - 8) = 9 - x + 24$

Remove the second set of parentheses. They serve no purpose in this equation, except to make it look more complicated than it really is.

$$x - 4x + 8 + 9 + 6x - 8 = 9 - x + 24$$

Using addition and subtraction, move all terms containing x to the left side, and all pure numbers to the right side.

$$x - 4x + 6x + x = 9 + 24 - 8 - 9 + 8$$

Performing the indicated additions and subtractions gives

$$4x = 24.$$

Dividing both sides by 4 gives

$$x = 6.$$

So, the correct answer is (D).

PROBLEM I.17

$\frac{2}{3} + \frac{5}{9} =$

(A) $\dfrac{7}{12}$

(D) $\dfrac{7}{9}$

(B) $\dfrac{11}{9}$

(E) $\dfrac{11}{3}$

(C) $\dfrac{7}{3}$

SOLUTION

(B)   A common denominator is needed to add fractions.

The least common denominator in this problem is 9, since the smallest number that both 3 and 9 will divide into is 9.

$$\frac{2}{3} + \frac{5}{9} = \left[\left(\frac{2}{3} \right) \times \left(\frac{3}{3} \right) \right] + \frac{5}{9}$$

(Within the brackets, we are converting $\frac{2}{3}$ to ninths)

$$= \left[\frac{2 \times 3}{3 \times 3} \right] + \frac{5}{9}$$

$$= \frac{6}{9} + \frac{5}{9}$$

$$= \frac{6+5}{9}$$

$$= \frac{11}{9}$$

So, the correct answer is (B).

■ PROBLEM I.18

Add $\frac{3}{6} + \frac{2}{6}$.

(A) $\dfrac{1}{12}$ (D) $\dfrac{8}{9}$

(B) $\dfrac{5}{6}$ (E) $\dfrac{9}{8}$

(C) $\dfrac{5}{12}$

SOLUTION

(B)   The given fractions already have the same denominator, so they are ready to be added.

$$\frac{3}{6} + \frac{2}{6} = \frac{3+2}{6}$$

$$= \frac{5}{6}$$

So, the correct answer is (B).

■ PROBLEM I.19

A plumber used pieces of pipe measuring $4\frac{1}{4}$ feet, $2\frac{2}{3}$ feet, and $3\frac{1}{2}$ feet. If the pieces of pipe were cut from a 15-foot length of pipe, how many feet of pipe remain? Disregard waste.

(A) $4\dfrac{7}{12}$ ft   (D) $10\dfrac{5}{12}$ ft

(B) $5\dfrac{1}{6}$ ft   (E) $11\dfrac{1}{3}$ ft

(C) $9\dfrac{5}{6}$ ft

SOLUTION

(A)   We want to find how many feet of pipe are left after several pieces have been cut off.

feet of pipe remaining = (original length of pipe)
– (lengths of cut off pieces)

$$\text{feet of pipe remaining} = (15) - \left(4\frac{1}{4} + 2\frac{2}{3} + 3\frac{1}{2}\right)$$

Let's start by finding the sum
$$\left(4\frac{1}{4} + 2\frac{2}{3} + 3\frac{1}{2}\right).$$

(Later, we will come back and subtract it from 15.)
$$\left(4\frac{1}{4} + 2\frac{2}{3} + 3\frac{1}{2}\right)$$

(Given sum)

$$= \left[\left(4 + \frac{1}{4}\right) + \left(2 + \frac{2}{3}\right) + \left(3 + \frac{1}{2}\right)\right]$$

(Broke up mixed numbers into whole and fractional parts)

$$= (4 + 2 + 3) + \left(\frac{1}{4} + \frac{2}{3} + \frac{1}{2}\right)$$

(Regrouped terms)

$$= (9) + \left(\frac{1}{4} + \frac{2}{3} + \frac{1}{2} \right)$$

(Added terms in first set of parentheses)

$$= 9 + \left[\left(\frac{1}{4} \times \frac{3}{3} \right) + \left(\frac{2}{3} \times \frac{4}{4} \right) + \left(\frac{1}{2} \times \frac{6}{6} \right) \right]$$

(Changed fractions to common denominator, which is 12)

$$= 9 + \left(\frac{3}{12} + \frac{8}{12} + \frac{6}{12} \right)$$

$$= 9 + \left(\frac{17}{12} \right)$$

(Added fractions)

$$= 9 + \left(\frac{12}{12} + \frac{5}{12} \right)$$

(Rewrote $\frac{17}{12}$)

$$= 9 + \left(1 + \frac{5}{12} \right)$$

(Replaced $\frac{12}{12}$ by 1)

$$= 10 + \frac{5}{12}$$

$$= 10 \frac{5}{12}$$

Now, substitute $10\frac{5}{12}$ back into the original equation.

$$\text{Remaining length of pipe} = 15 - 10\frac{5}{12}$$

$$= 14\frac{12}{12} - 10\frac{5}{12}$$

(Borrowed $\frac{12}{12}$ from 15)

$$= 4\frac{7}{12} \text{ feet}$$

(Subtracted 10 from 14, and $\frac{5}{12}$ from $\frac{12}{12}$)

So, the correct answer is (A).

■ PROBLEM I.20

Peter has five rulers of 30 cm each and three of 20 cm each. What is the average length of Peter's rulers?

(A) 25   (D) 26.25

(B) 27   (E) 27.25

(C) 23

SOLUTION

(D)   We apply the definition of the average to our problem.

$$\text{Average} = \frac{\text{sum of the lengths of all the rulers}}{\text{how many rulers there are}}$$

$$= \frac{30 + 30 + 30 + 30 + 30 + 20 + 20 + 20}{8}$$

$$= \frac{(30 \times 5) + (20 \times 3)}{8}$$

$$= \frac{150 + 60}{8}$$

$$= \frac{210}{8}$$

$$= 26.25 \text{ cm}$$

So, the correct answer is (D).

■ PROBLEM I.21

If $2^{(6x-8)} = 16$, then $x =$

(A) 2.   (D) 1.

(B) 4.   (E) 6.

(C) 10.

SOLUTION

(A)   First, note that $16 = 2^4$.

(Verify this for yourself: $2^4 = 2 \times 2 \times 2 \times 2 = 16$.)

Next, substitute 2^4 for 16 in the given equation.

$$2^{(6x-8)} = 16 \quad \text{(Given)}$$

$$2^{(6x-8)} = 2^4 \quad \text{(Substituted for 16)}$$

We are now in a position to *equate the exponents* (set the exponent from the left side equal to the exponent from the right side).

$$6x - 8 = 4$$

Solve for x:

$$6x = 4 + 8$$

$$6x = 12$$

$$x = \frac{12}{6}$$

$$x = 2$$

So, the correct answer is (A).

■ PROBLEM I.22

Three times the first of three consecutive odd integers is three more than twice the third. What is the second of the three consecutive odd integers?

(A) 7

(B) 9

(C) 11

(D) 13

(E) 15

SOLUTION

(D)   Three consecutive odd integers can be written as

$$x = \text{first odd integer}$$

$$x + 2 = \text{second odd integer}$$

$$x + 4 = \text{third odd integer}$$

Now, we must translate the word problem into its mathematical equivalent. Follow closely how each word in the problem is replaced by a number or symbol.

(three) (times) (the first) (is) (three) (more than) (twice) (the third)

$$3 \quad \times \quad x \quad = \quad 3 \quad + \quad 2\times \quad (x+4)$$

or, $\qquad 3x = 3 + 2(x + 4)$

Using the distributive property we get

$$3x = 3 + 2x + 8.$$

Collecting like terms on the left gives

$$3x - 2x = 3 + 8$$

$$x = 11 \text{ (first odd integer)}$$

We have just found the first odd integer, x, but the problem asks for the *second* odd integer.

$$\text{second odd integer} = x + 2 = 11 + 2 = 13$$

So, the correct answer is (D).

■ PROBLEM I.23

The length of a rectangle is four more than twice the width. The perimeter of the rectangle is 44 meters. Find the length.

(A) 6 m

(B) 8 m

(C) 11 m

(D) 16 m

(E) 22 m

SOLUTION

(D) Let l = length

$\qquad w$ = width

Translate the given information into an equation.

(length) (is) (four) (more than) (twice) (the width)

$$l \quad = \quad 4 \quad + \quad 2\times \quad w$$

or, $l = 4 + 2w$ (1)

We will soon plug this relation into the perimeter equation.

perimeter $= 44 = l + l + w + w$.

Substituting $(4 + 2w)$ for l, from equation (1), gives.

perimeter $= 44 = (4 + 2w) + (4 + 2w) + w + w$

$$= 4 + 2w + 4 + 2w + w + w$$

$$= 6w + 8$$

or, $44 = 6w + 8$

Solve for w.

$$44 - 8 = 6w$$

$$36 = 6w$$

$$w = \frac{36}{6}$$

$$w = 6$$

We have just found the width, w, but the problem asks for length. To find the length, use equation (1).

$$l = 4 + 2w$$

$$= 4 + (2)(6) \quad \text{(Substituted 6 for } w)$$

$$= 4 + 12$$

$$= 16$$

The length is 16 meters.

So, the correct answer is (D).

▪ PROBLEM I.24

John bought a $250 radio. The salesman gave him a 10% discount. How much did he pay for the radio?

(A) $25

(B) $125

(C) $175

(D) $225

(E) $275

SOLUTION

(**D**)   John bought the radio at a discount, so he payed *less* than the original price.

First, find the discount.

discount = 10% of original price

$$= .10 \times 250 \qquad \text{(Wrote 10\% in decimal form)}$$

$$= \$25$$

Next, put the value we just found for the discount into the following equation:

$$\text{(Original price)} - \text{(discount)} = \text{(price John payed)}$$

$$(250) - (25) = \text{(price John payed)}$$

$$\$225 = \text{price John payed}$$

So, the correct answer is (D).

■ PROBLEM I.25

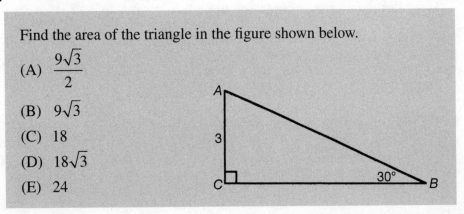

Find the area of the triangle in the figure shown below.

(A) $\dfrac{9\sqrt{3}}{2}$

(B) $9\sqrt{3}$

(C) 18

(D) $18\sqrt{3}$

(E) 24

SOLUTION

(**A**)   *For a triangle:*

$$\text{Area} = \tfrac{1}{2} \times \text{base} \times \text{height}$$

$$= \tfrac{1}{2} bh$$

To use this formula, we need to know h and b. We do know h ($h = 3$, from the diagram).

However, we cannot apply the formula until we find b.

To find b (length of the base):

(a)   Note that the triangle pictured is a $30 - 60 - 90$ triangle.

(b)   Recall that the lengths of the sides of a $30 - 60 - 90$ triangle are in the ratio $1 : \sqrt{3} : 2$. (This gives just the ratio of their lengths, not their actual lengths.)

(c)   To find the actual lengths of the sides for the pictured triangle, multiply the ratio through by 3 (since our smallest side has a length of 3, not a length of 1).

$$3 \times (1 : \sqrt{3} : 2) = (3 \times 1) : (3 \times \sqrt{3}) : (3 \times 2)$$
$$= 3 : 3\sqrt{3} : 6$$

This tells us that for our particular triangle:

length of the smaller side $= 3$

length of the larger side (the base) $= 3\sqrt{3}$

length of the hypotenuse $= 6$

Thus, the quantity we were trying to find, b, is equal to $3\sqrt{3}$.

(We do not need to know the hypotenuse for this problem, but it was shown here for the sake of completeness).

Find the area:

$$\text{Area} = \tfrac{1}{2}bh$$
$$= \tfrac{1}{2}(3\sqrt{3})(3) \qquad \text{(Substituted for } b \text{ and } h)$$
$$= \frac{9\sqrt{3}}{2}$$

So, the correct answer is (A).

■ PROBLEM I.26

I filled $\frac{2}{3}$ of my swimming pool with 1,800 ft³. What is the total capacity of my swimming pool?

(A) 2,400 ft³

(D) 3,600 ft³

(B) 2,700 ft³

(E) 3,200 ft³

(C) 3,000 ft³

SOLUTION

(B)   We want to find how much water the swimming pool can hold when it is full. This is called the capacity of the swimming pool.

Given:

$$\frac{2}{3} \times (\text{capacity of swimming pool}) = 1,800$$

Solve:

$$(\text{capacity of swimming pool}) = 1,800 \times \frac{3}{2}$$

$$= \frac{1,800 \times 3}{2}$$

$$= 2,700 \text{ ft}^3$$

So, the correct answer is (B).

■ PROBLEM I.27

A jug will hold $\frac{2}{3}$ gallon of punch. How much punch is in the jug when it is $\frac{3}{4}$ full?

(A) $\frac{5}{7}$ gallon

(D) $\frac{2}{3}$ gallon

(B) $\frac{1}{2}$ gallon

(E) $\frac{1}{12}$ gallon

(C) $\frac{1}{4}$ gallon

SOLUTION

(B)   Note that a *full* jug contains $\frac{2}{3}$ gallon.

Thus, $\frac{3}{4}$ of a full jug

$$= \frac{3}{4} \times \frac{2}{3} \text{ gallon}$$

(Replaced "full jug" by $\frac{2}{3}$ gallon)

$$= \frac{6}{12} \text{ gallon}$$

$$= \frac{1}{2} \text{ gallon}$$

So, the correct answer is (B).

◼ PROBLEM I.28

If $f(x) = x + 1$, $g(x) = 2x - 3$, and an operation * is defined *for* all real numbers a and b by the equation $a * b = 2a + b - ab$, then $f(3) * g(4) =$

(A) –9.   (D) 0.

(B) –7.   (E) 5.

(C) –1.

SOLUTION

(B)   Here's our plan:

Step I—Find $f(3)$ and $g(4)$.

Step II—Use these values to find $f(3) * g(4)$, where * is defined in the problem.

Step I

(a) $f(x) = x + 1$

       $f(3) = 3 + 1$ (Substituted 3 for x)

So, $f(3) = 4$

(b) $g(x) = 2x - 3$

$g(4) = (2)(4) - 3$ (Substituted 4 for x)

$g(4) = 8 - 3$

So, $g(4) = 5$

Step II

We want to find $f(3) * g(4)$.

We have a formula for $a * b$.

For use in the formula, assign the following:

$a = f(3) = 4$

$b = g(4) = 5$

Then replace each "a" in the formula with 4 and each "b" with 5.

$f(3) * g(4) = a * b$

$= 2a + b - ab$

$= 2(4) + 5 - 4 \times 5$ (Substituted $a = 4$, $b = 5$)

$= 8 + 5 - 20$

$= 13 - 20$

$= -7$

So, the correct answer is (B).

■ PROBLEM I.29

What is the value(s) of x in the equation $(4x - 3)^2 = 4$?

(A) $\dfrac{5}{4}$ (D) $\dfrac{1}{4}, \dfrac{5}{2}$

(B) $\dfrac{1}{4}$ (E) $\dfrac{5}{2}, \dfrac{1}{5}$

(C) $\dfrac{5}{4}, \dfrac{1}{4}$

SOLUTION

(C)   We are given the equation $(4x - 3)^2 = 4$.

Take the square root of both sides to get the following two equations:

$$\sqrt{(4x+3)^2} = \sqrt{4} \qquad \sqrt{(4x+3)^2} = -\sqrt{4}$$

$$4x - 3 = 2 \qquad\qquad 4x - 3 = -2$$

$$4x = 2 + 3 \qquad\qquad 4x = -2 + 3$$

$$x = \frac{5}{4} \qquad \text{or} \qquad x = \frac{1}{4}$$

Thus, there are two different values of x which, if plugged into the original equation $(4x - 3)^2 = 4$, will make the equation true.

The correct answer is (C).

■ PROBLEM I.30

Fifteen percent of what number is 60?

(A) 9   (D) 200

(B) 51   (E) 400

(C) 69

SOLUTION

(E)   Translate the given information into an equation.

(fifteen percent) (of) (what number) (is) 60

.15   × x = 60

or, $.15x = 60$

Solve for x.

$$x = \frac{60}{.15}$$

$$= 400$$

So, the correct answer is (E).

■ PROBLEM I.31

$10^3 + 10^5 =$

(A) 10^8 (D) 2^{15}

(B) 10^{15} (E) $101,000$

(C) 20^8

SOLUTION

(E) $10^3 + 10^5 = (10)(10)(10) + (10)(10)(10)(10)(10)$

$$= 1,000 + 100,000$$

$$= 101,000$$

So, the correct answer is (E).

■ PROBLEM I.32

If $a = 4$ and $b = 7$, then $\dfrac{a + \frac{a}{b}}{a - \frac{a}{b}}$

(A) $\dfrac{3}{4}$.   (D) $\dfrac{4}{3}$.

(B) $\dfrac{3}{7}$.   (E) $\dfrac{7}{3}$.

(C) 1.

SOLUTION

(D)   Every place you see an "a," substitute 4.

Every place you see a "b," substitute 7.

$$\frac{a + \frac{a}{b}}{a - \frac{a}{b}}$$

(Given)

$$= \frac{4 + \frac{4}{7}}{4 - \frac{4}{7}}$$

(Substituted $a = 4$ and $b = 7$)

$$= \frac{\left[4 \times \left(\frac{7}{7}\right)\right] + \frac{4}{7}}{\left[4 \times \left(\frac{7}{7}\right)\right] - \frac{4}{7}}$$

(In the brackets, we are finding how many sevenths the number 4 is equal to.)

$$= \frac{\frac{28}{7} + \frac{4}{7}}{\frac{28}{7} - \frac{4}{7}}$$

(Inside the brackets, we found that $4 = \frac{28}{7}$.)

$$= \frac{\frac{32}{7}}{\frac{24}{7}}$$

$$= \frac{32}{7} \times \frac{7}{24}$$

(Used the fact that $\frac{\frac{a}{b}}{\frac{c}{d}} = \frac{a}{b} \times \frac{d}{c}$)

$$= \frac{32}{24}$$

$$= \frac{4}{3}$$

So, the correct answer is (D).

■ PROBLEM I.33

The greatest area that a rectangle whose perimeter is 52 m can have is

(A) 12 m².   (D) 168 m².

(B) 169 m².   (E) 52 m².

(C) 172 m².

SOLUTION

(B) *You need these facts to understand which rectangle to use:*

(1) Some rectangles are long and thin; others are closer to being square; (also a square is itself a rectangle).

(2) It is possible to find several differently shaped rectangles that have the same perimeter, but different area.

(3) It turns out that a *square* encompasses a greater area than any longer, thinner rectangle with the same perimeter (square gives maximum area).

(4) The problem asks for "greatest area," so our rectangle must be a square.

Find the length of a side:

$$\text{length of one side} = \frac{\text{perimeter}}{4}$$

(For a square, lengths of sides are equal; divide perimeter into four equal parts.)

$$= \frac{52}{4}$$

$$= 13 \text{ m}$$

Find the area:

$$\text{Area} = \text{length} \times \text{width}$$

$$= 13 \times 13$$

(Length and width are equal for a square.)

$$= 169 \text{ m}^2$$

So, the correct answer is (B).

PROBLEM I.34

The number 120 is separated into two parts. The larger part exceeds three times the smaller by 12. The smaller part is

(A) 27.

(B) 33.

(C) 15.

(D) 39.

(E) 29.

SOLUTION

(A)   Separate the number 120 into two parts.

$$x = \text{larger part}$$

$$120 - x = \text{smaller part}$$

(larger part + smaller part = 120; so, 120 − larger part = smaller part)

Translate the given information into an equation.

(The larger part) = (three times) (the smaller part) + 12

$$\begin{array}{ccccc} 1 & = & 3 \times & (120 - x) & + 12 \end{array}$$

or, $x = 3(120 - x) + 12$

Using the distributive property gives

$$x = (3)(120) - 3x + 12$$

$$x = 360 - 3x + 12$$

Move all terms containing x to the left side and all pure numbers to the right side to give

$$x + 3x = 360 + 12$$

$$4x = 372$$

$$x = \frac{372}{4}$$

$$x = 93 \quad \text{(Larger part)}$$

The question asks for the *smaller* part.

$$\text{smaller part} = 120 - x$$

$$= 120 - 93$$

(Substituted for x, from above)

$$= 27$$

So, the correct answer is (A).

■ PROBLEM I.35

Of the following relations, the ones that are functions are:

I. $\dfrac{x^2}{81} - \dfrac{y^2}{16} = 3$

II. $x^2 + \left| \dfrac{\sqrt{y^2}}{3} \right| = 3y$

III. $y = \sqrt{3}x$

(A) I only.   (D) I, II, and III.

(B) I and III only.   (E) II and III only.

(C) II only.

SOLUTION

(E)   *To determine if a relation is a function:*

(1)   Solve for *y* if possible.

(2)   Use the following test:

If there is *only one y* value for each *x* value: *Yes*, a function.

If there is *more than one y* value for any *x* value: *No*, not a function.

Now, let's test each of the given relations:

I. $\dfrac{x^2}{81} - \dfrac{y^2}{16} = 3$

It would be too time consuming to solve this exactly, and anyway it is not necessary. We are only interested in the relationship between *x* and *y*, so we don't care what the constants are.

We rewrite the equation, showing the essential features.

$x^2 - y^2 =$ some known constants

We'll get tired of writing "some known constants," so let's just write "*k*."

$$x^2 - y^2 = k$$
$$-y^2 = k - x^2$$
$$y^2 = x^2 - k$$
$$y = \pm\sqrt{x^2 - k}$$

Imagine now that you plug in an x value on the right side. You'll see that there is *more than one* value of y for a given x.

These y values are

$$y = +\sqrt{x^2 - k} \text{ and } y = -\sqrt{x^2 - k}.$$

Thus, part I is *not* a function.

II. $$x^2 + \left|\frac{\sqrt{y^2}}{3}\right| = 3y$$

This one could trick you. If you spotted the x^2 and y^2, you might mistakenly assume that this is just like the last problem. It's not. Here the $\sqrt{y^2}$ simplifies down to just y to give

$$x^2 + \left|\frac{y}{3}\right| = 3y.$$

Note that y is positive (or zero), since we obtained it by taking a square root. (The symbol $\sqrt{}$ indicates the *positive* square root.) Recall also that the absolute value of a *positive* number is that number.

Thus, $\left|\dfrac{y}{3}\right| = \dfrac{y}{3}$ for this problem.

Removing the absolute value sign gives:

$$x^2 + \frac{y}{3} = 3y$$

$$3y - \frac{y}{3} = x^2$$

$$\frac{9y}{3} - \frac{y}{3} = x^2$$

$$\frac{8y}{3} = x^2$$

$$y = \frac{3}{8}x^2$$

Let's apply our function test. Imagine that you plug in some value of x on the right side. This value will be squared and then multiplied by $\frac{3}{8}$ to give a *single y* value. Since there is *only one y* value for a given x, part II is a function.

III. $y = \sqrt{3}x$

This one is easy—it's already in the form we need. Each x value gets multiplied by $\sqrt{3}$ to give *one y* value. Part III is thus a function.

We have shown that only parts II and III are functions.

So, the correct answer is (E).

Note: If you were to draw the graphs for these equations you would find

Part I—a hyperbola

Part II—a parabola

Part III—a straight line

■ PROBLEM I.36

Two pounds of pears and one pound of peaches cost $1.40. Three pounds of pears and two pounds of peaches cost $2.40. How much is the combined cost of one pound of pears and one pound of peaches?

(A) $2.00   (D) $.80

(B) $1.50   (E) $1.00

(C) $1.60

SOLUTION

(E)   To solve this problem we must set up a simultaneous equation.

Let $x =$ the cost of one pound of pears

$2x =$ the cost of two pounds of pears

Let $y =$ the cost of one pound of peaches

$2x + y = 1.40$ (1)

Similarly, we have

$3x =$ the cost of three pounds of pears

$2y =$ the cost of two pounds of peaches

$3x + 2y = 2.40$ (2)

Equations (1) and (2) are solved simultaneously as follows:

$2x + 2x + y = 1.40$ (1)

$3x + 3x + 2y = 2.40$ (2)

In equation (1) we solve for y in terms of x.

$2x + y = 1.40$

$y = 1.40 - 2x$

We then substitute $y = 1.40 - 2x$ for y in equation (2).

$3x + 2y = 2.40$

$3x + 2(1.40 - 2x) = 2.40$

Solving this equation for x we obtain the following.

$3x + 2(1.40 - 2x) = 2.40$

$3x + 2.80 - 4x = 2.40$

$-1x = -.40$

$x = .40$

Thus, one pound of pears cost $.40.

Substituting $.40 for the value of x in equation (1), we can obtain the value of y.

$2(.40) + y = 1.40$

$.80 + y = 1.40$

$y = .60$

Therefore, the cost of one pound of pears and one pound of peaches is $.40 + .60 = 1.00$.

The correct choice is (E).

PROBLEM I.37

The length of a rectangle is $6L$ and the width is $4W$. What is the perimeter?

(A) $12L + 8W$ (D) $20LW$

(B) $12L^2 + 8W^2$ (E) $24LW$

(C) $6L + 4W$

SOLUTION

(A)   The perimeter of a rectangle is equal to the sum of its sides.

The perimeter is equal to $2 \times$ (length) plus $2 \times$ (width).

Therefore, the perimeter equals

$2(6L) + 2(4W) = 12L + 8W.$

The correct answer is (A).

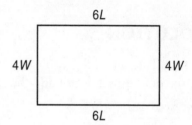

PROBLEM I.38

Using order of operations, solve: $3 \times 6 - 12 \div 2$.

(A) -9.   (D) 12.

(B) 3.   (E) 18.

(C) 6.

SOLUTION

(D)   According to the order of operations, we perform all multiplication and division first from left to right. Then additions and subtractions are performed from left to right.

$$3 \times 6 - 12 \div 2 = 18 - 12 \div 2$$

$$= 18 - 6$$

$$= 12$$

The correct answer is (D).

■ PROBLEM I.39

Change $4\frac{5}{6}$ to an improper fraction.

(A) $\dfrac{5}{24}$

(D) $\dfrac{30}{4}$

(B) $\dfrac{9}{6}$

(E) $\dfrac{120}{6}$

(C) $\dfrac{29}{6}$

SOLUTION

(C)   To change $4\frac{5}{6}$ to an improper fraction, we multiply the whole number by the denominator and add the numerator.

$$\frac{4(6)+5}{6}=\frac{29}{6}$$

The correct answer is (C).

■ PROBLEM I.40

Find the sum of

$$5\tfrac{3}{4}, 2\tfrac{11}{16}, \text{ and } 7\tfrac{1}{8}.$$

(A) $14\dfrac{8}{17}$

(D) $15\dfrac{15}{28}$

(B) $14\dfrac{15}{16}$

(E) $15\dfrac{9}{16}$

(C) $15\dfrac{1}{2}$

SOLUTION

(E)   To find the sum of these numbers, we must first find a common denominator for the fractional component.

$$\frac{3}{4} = \frac{12}{16}$$

$$\frac{11}{16} = \frac{11}{16}$$

$$\frac{1}{8} = \frac{2}{16}$$

16 is the lowest common denominator (LCD). Therefore,

$$5\frac{3}{4} = 5\frac{12}{16}$$

$$2\frac{11}{16} = 2\frac{11}{16}$$

$$7\frac{1}{8} = 7\frac{2}{16}$$

We then add the whole numbers and the fractional components.

$$5\frac{12}{16} + 2\frac{11}{16} + 7\frac{2}{16} = 14\frac{25}{16}$$

$14\frac{25}{16}$ can be reduced to $15\frac{9}{16}$.

The correct answer is (E).

PROBLEM I.41

A counting number with exactly two different factors is called a prime number. Which of the following pairs of numbers are consecutive prime numbers?

(A) 27 and 29   (D) 37 and 29

(B) 31 and 33   (E) 41 and 43

(C) 35 and 37

SOLUTION

(E)   A prime number is a number that is divisible by one and itself only.

Analyzing the choices, we can see that in choices (A), (B), and (C) at least one of the numbers in each pair is not a prime number.

In choice (A), $27 = 9 \times 3$, 29 is prime.

In choice (B), $33 = 3 \times 11$, 31 is prime.

In choice (C), $35 = 5 \times 7$, 37 is prime.

In choice (D), both numbers are prime, but they are not consecutive.

In answer (E), 41 and 43 are both prime numbers and consecutive numbers that are prime.

■ PROBLEM I.42

What part of three-fourths is one-tenth?

(A) $\dfrac{1}{8}$

(D) $\dfrac{3}{40}$

(B) $\dfrac{15}{2}$

(E) $\dfrac{3}{30}$

(C) $\dfrac{2}{15}$

SOLUTION

(C)   We must translate the statement into an equation:

(What part) (of) (three-fourths) (is) (one-tenth)

$$x \quad \times \quad \frac{3}{4} \quad = \quad \frac{1}{10}$$

or, $\dfrac{3}{4}x = \dfrac{1}{10}$

Solve for x,

$$x = \frac{\frac{1}{10}}{\frac{3}{4}} = \frac{1}{10} \times \frac{4}{3}$$

Dividing by a fraction is the same as multiplying by its reciprocal. We multiply $\frac{1}{10}$ by the reciprocal of $\frac{3}{4}$, which is $\frac{4}{3}$.

$$\frac{1}{10} \times \frac{4}{3} = \frac{4}{30}$$

$$= \frac{2}{15}$$

The correct choice is (C).

■ PROBLEM I.43

Change the fraction $\frac{7}{8}$ to a decimal.

(A) .666

(D) .875

(B) .75

(E) 1.142

(C) .777

SOLUTION

(D)   To change a fraction to a decimal divide the numerator, 7, by the denominator, 8. Add a decimal point after the 7 and the necessary zeros and continue dividing.

```
        .875
  8⟌ 7.000
    −64
     .60
    −56
     .40
    −40
      0
```

The correct choice is (D).

■ PROBLEM I.44

Twelve more than twice a number is 31 less than three times the number. Find the number.

(A) − 43

(D) 19

(B) − 19

(E) 43

(C) − 9

SOLUTION

(E)   Let $x =$ the number

We must convert the sentence into an equation.

$$2x + 12 = 3x - 31$$

Now we solve for x by subtracting $2x$ from both sides.

$$-2x + 2x + 12 = 3x - 31 - 2x$$

$$12 = x - 31$$

Adding 31 to both sides we get

$$43 = x.$$

The correct answer is (E).

◼ PROBLEM I.45

The area of Jane's living room is 48 m². The length of the room is 2 m more than the width. What is the length?

(A) 4 m   (D) 10 m

(B) 6 m   (E) 12 m

(C) 8 m

SOLUTION

(C)   Let $w =$ width of the room

$l =$ length of the room

Since the length is 2 more than the width,

$$l = (w + 2)$$

Using the formula for area (area = length × width) and substituting the above information, we get

$$(w + 2)\, w = 48$$

$$w^2 + 2w = 48$$

$$w^2 + 2w - 48 = 0$$

Factoring this equation, we obtain

$(w + 8)(w - 6) = 0.$

Setting each partial product to zero,

$w + 8 = 0 \qquad\qquad w - 6 = 0$

$\qquad w = -8 \qquad\qquad\quad w = 6$

Although there are two possible solutions for w, there cannot be a negative value for a room dimension. Therefore, $w = 6$ and $l = w + 2 = 6 + 2 = 8$.

The correct choice is (C).

■ PROBLEM I.46

Ron saves \$38 in four weeks. How many weeks will it take Ron to save \$152 at the same rate?

(A) 12   (D) 18

(B) 14   (E) 20

(C) 16

SOLUTION

(C)   Ron saves \$38 in 4 weeks.

We can find the number of weeks it will take Ron to save \$152 by setting up a proportion.

$$\frac{\$38}{4 \text{ weeks}} = \frac{\$152}{x \text{ weeks}}$$

We can solve for x by cross multiplying.

$38x = 4(152)$

$38x = 608$

$x = \dfrac{608}{38}$

$x = 16$

The correct answer is (C).

◼ PROBLEM I.47

Find the area of a right triangle with a hypotenuse of 17 cm and a base of 8 cm.

(A) 45 cm²   (D) 120 cm²

(B) 60 cm²   (E) 138 cm²

(C) 68 cm²

SOLUTION

(B)   The area of a triangle is $\frac{1}{2}$ base × height. The base is 8 and the hypotenuse is 17. To find the height, we use the Pythagorean Theorem.

$$h^2 + 8^2 = 17^2$$

$$h^2 + 64 = 289$$

$$h^2 = 225$$

$$h = \sqrt{225}$$

$$h = 15$$

Now that we have $h = 15$, we can substitute this value and find the area of the triangle.

$$\text{Area} = \frac{1}{2}\,(\text{base})(\text{height})$$

$$\text{Area} = \frac{1}{2}\,(8 \text{ cm})(15 \text{ cm})$$

$$\text{Area} = 60 \text{ cm}^2$$

The correct choice is (B).

PROBLEM I.48

Find the cost of seeding a lawn shaped like a parallelogram with a base of 6 m and a height of 5 m. One kilogram of grass seed covers 15 m² and costs $7.50.

(A) $3.75   (D) $15.00

(B) $7.50   (E) $22.50

(C) $11.25

SOLUTION

(D)

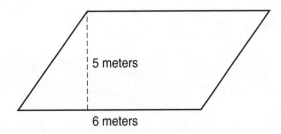

5 meters

6 meters

The area of a parallelogram = (base) (height)

Area = (6 m) (5 m) = 30 m²

One kilogram of grass seed covers 15 m² and costs $7.50. We would need two kilograms of grass seed to cover 30 m². This would cost 2 × $7.50 = $15.00.

The correct choice is (D).

PROBLEM 1.49

If the measure of an angle exceeds its complement by 40°, then its measure is

(A) 65°.   (D) 40°.

(B) 50°.   (E) 30°.

(C) 45°.

SOLUTION

(A)   Two angles that are complementary add up to 90°.

Let $x =$ the angle

$x - 40 =$ the complement

$$x + (x - 40) = 90$$

$$2x - 40 = 90$$

$$2x = 90 + 40$$

$$2x = 130$$

$$x = 65°$$

The correct choice is (A).

◼ PROBLEM I.50

Two dice are thrown, one red and one green. The probability that the number on the red exceeds the number showing on the green by exactly two is

(A) $\dfrac{1}{18}$.

(D) $\dfrac{1}{36}$.

(B) $\dfrac{1}{4}$.

(E) $\dfrac{1}{24}$.

(C) $\dfrac{1}{9}$.

SOLUTION

(C)   If two dice are thrown, there are six possibilities for each die (1, 2, 3, 4, 5, or 6). Therefore, there are $6^2 = 36$ possibilities for the total number of combinations on a pair of dice.

If the number on the red die exceeds the number on the green die by two, we have the following combinations possible.

Red	Green Combinations	
2	$2 - 2 = 0$ 0	
3	$3 - 2 = 1$ 1	3, 1
4	$4 - 2 = 2$ 2	4, 2
5	$5 - 2 = 3$ 3	5, 3
6	$6 - 2 = 4$ 4	6, 4

There are only four combinations out of 36 that satisfy the event that the number on the red die exceeds the number on the green die by 2. Hence, the probability for this event to happen is $\frac{4}{36} = \frac{1}{9}$.

The correct choice is (C).

◼ PROBLEM I.51

$$\sqrt{X\sqrt{X\sqrt{X}}} =$$

(A) $X^{\frac{7}{8}}$

(D) $X^{\frac{3}{4}}$

(B) $X^{\frac{7}{4}}$

(E) $X^{\frac{15}{8}}$

(C) $X^{\frac{15}{16}}$

SOLUTION

(A)   The best way to handle this problem is to simplify in steps.

$$\sqrt{X\sqrt{X\sqrt{X}}} = ?$$

Since $\sqrt{X} = X^{\frac{1}{2}}$ then

$$\sqrt{X\sqrt{X \times \sqrt{X}}} = \sqrt{X\sqrt{X \times X^{\frac{1}{2}}}}.$$

We can simplify $\sqrt{X \times X^{\frac{1}{2}}}$ by using 2 as a common denominator for the exponents.

Therefore,

$$\sqrt{X \times X^{\frac{1}{2}}} = \sqrt{X^{\frac{2}{2}} \times X^{\frac{1}{2}}}$$

$$= \sqrt{X^{\frac{3}{2}}}$$

$$= \left(X^{\frac{3}{2}}\right)^{\frac{1}{2}}$$

$$= X^{\frac{3}{4}}$$

Going back to the original problem, we have

$$\sqrt{X\sqrt{X^{\frac{3}{2}}}} = \sqrt{X \times X^{\frac{3}{4}}}.$$

Using 4 as a common denominator of the exponents, we can simplify again.

$$\sqrt{X^{\frac{4}{4}} \times X^{\frac{3}{4}}} = \sqrt{X^{\frac{7}{4}}}$$

$$= \left(X^{\frac{7}{4}}\right)^{\frac{1}{2}}$$

$$= X^{\frac{7}{8}}$$

The correct choice is (A).

■ PROBLEM I.52

A line segment is drawn from the point (3, 5) to the point (9, 13). What are the coordinates of the midpoint of the line segment?

(A) (9, 6)   (D) (12, 18)

(B) (6, 9)   (E) (6, 8)

(C) (3, 4)

SOLUTION

(B)   If two points on a line segment are (x_1, y_1) and (x_2, y_2), then the midpoint between these two points is given by

$$\left(\frac{x_1 + x_2}{2}, \frac{y_1 + y_2}{2}\right).$$

If we consider the line segment connecting the points $(3, 5)$ to $(9, 13)$, then

$$x_1 = 3 \qquad\qquad x_2 = 9$$

$$y_1 = 5 \qquad\qquad y_2 = 13$$

Therefore, the midpoint of the line segment is

$$\left(\frac{3+9}{2}, \frac{5+13}{2}\right) = \left(\frac{12}{2}, \frac{18}{2}\right)$$

$$= (6, 9)$$

The correct choice is (B).

■ PROBLEM I.53

The number missing in the series 2, 6, 12, 20, x, 42, 56 is

(A) 36.   (D) 38.

(B) 24.   (E) 40.

(C) 30.

SOLUTION

(C) We note the following pattern arithmetically by considering the following differences:

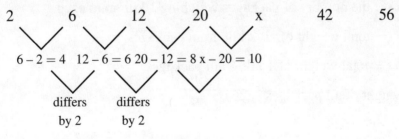

Then $x - 20 = 10$ in keeping with the pattern

Solving for x,

$$x - 20 = 10$$

$$x = 30$$

To check the answer, analyze the pattern with $x = 30$.

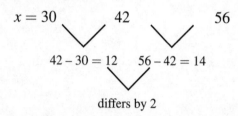

We see that the pattern continues. Therefore, the missing piece is 30.

The correct choice is (C).

■ PROBLEM I.54

A truck contains 150 small packages, some weighing 1 kg each and some weighing 2 kg each. How many packages weighing 2 kg each are in the truck if the total weight of all the packages is 264 kg?

(A) 36   (D) 124

(B) 52   (E) 114

(C) 88

SOLUTION

(E)   Let (x) = the number of packages weighing 2 kilograms each.

$(150 - x)$ = the number of packages weighing 1 kilogram each.

$2(x)$ = total weight of all 2 kilogram packages.

$1(150 - x)$ = total weight of 1 kilogram packages.

The total weight of all packages is 264.

$$2x + (150 - x) = 264$$

Combining like terms, we can simplify.

$$2x + 150 - x = 264$$

$$x + 150 = 264$$

$$x = 264 - 150$$

$$x = 114$$

There are 114 packages weighing 2 kilograms each.

The correct choice is (E).

■ PROBLEM I.55

The solution of the equation $4 - 5(2y + 4) = 4$ is

(A) $-\dfrac{2}{5}$.

(D) -2.

(B) 8.

(E) -3.

(C) 4.

SOLUTION

(D) $4 - 5(2y + 4) = 4$

To solve the problem we first apply the distribution law to obtain the following:

$$4 - 10y - 20 = 4$$

We can further simplify by combining numerical terms on the left side.

$$-10y - 16 = 4$$

Combining numerical terms and solving for y, we get

$$-10y = 20$$

$$\frac{-10y}{-10} = \frac{20}{-10}$$

$$y = -2$$

The correct answer is (D).

PROBLEM 1.56

What is the product of $(\sqrt{3} + 6)$ and $(\sqrt{3} - 2)$?

(A) $9 + 4\sqrt{3}$ 　　　　　　　　　　(D) $-9 + 2\sqrt{3}$

(B) -9 　　　　　　　　　　　　　　(E) 9

(C) $-9 + 4\sqrt{3}$

SOLUTION

(C) $\quad \left(\sqrt{3}+6\right)\left(\sqrt{3}-2\right) = \left(\sqrt{3}+6\right)\left(\sqrt{3}\right) - \left(\sqrt{3}+6\right)(2)$

$$= \sqrt{9} + 6\sqrt{3} - 2\sqrt{3} - 12$$
$$= 3 + 6\sqrt{3} - 2\sqrt{3} - 12$$
$$= -9 + 4\sqrt{3}$$

The correct choice is (C).

PROBLEM I.57

Two cyclists start toward each other from two towns that are 135 miles apart. One cyclist rides at 15 mph and the other rides at 12 mph. In how many hours will they meet?

(A) 3 　　　　　　　　　　　　　　(D) 11

(B) 5 　　　　　　　　　　　　　　(E) 15

(C) 9

SOLUTION

(B)　Let $x = $ the number of hours it takes for the two cyclists to meet

Distance $=$ rate $\times$ time

The cyclist who rides at 15 mph will travel a total of $15x$ miles.

The cyclist who rides at 12 mph will travel a total of $12x$ miles.

The total distance traveled is 135 miles.

We therefore add the distance traveled by both cyclists to obtain

$$12x + 15x = 135$$

$$27x = 135$$

$$x = \frac{135}{27}$$

$$x = 5$$

Therefore, the two cyclists will meet in 5 hours.

The correct choice is (B).

■ PROBLEM I.58

In rhombus *ABCD*, which of the following are true?

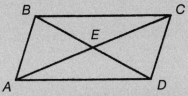

I.   ∠*BAE* and ∠*ECD* are congruent.
II. ∠*ADE* and ∠*CDE* are congruent.
III. ∠*ABE* and ∠*ADE* are congruent.

(A) I only.   (D) I and III only.

(B) II only.   (E) I, II, and III.

(C) I and II only.

SOLUTION

(E)   A rhombus is a parallelogram in which all four sides are the same length and the opposite sides are parallel. The diagonals of a rhombus bisect its angles. In the diagram sides $\overline{BA}$ and $\overline{CD}$ are parallel.

I. ∠*BAE* and ∠*ECD* are congruent since they are alternate interior angles of the parallel sides of the rhombus with $\overline{AC}$ as the transversal.

II. ∠*ADE* and ∠*CDE* are congruent since the diagonals of a rhombus bisect the angles of a rhombus.

III. ∠*ABE* and ∠*ADE* are congruent since $\overline{AB}$ is congruent to $\overline{AD}$ where $\overline{AB}$ and $\overline{AD}$ are sides of the rhombus. Triangle *ABD* is isosceles. Therefore the angles opposite these congruent sides are congruent.

The correct choice is (E).

■ PROBLEM I.59

If the length of segment $\overline{EB}$, base of triangle EBC, is equal to $\frac{1}{4}$ the length of segment $\overline{AB}$ ($\overline{AB}$ is the length of rectangle $ABCD$), and the area of triangle EBC is 12 square units, find the area of the shaded region.

(A) 24 square units

(B) 96 square units

(C) 84 square units

(D) 72 square units

(E) 120 square units

SOLUTION

(C) Let ($\overline{AB}$) represent the length of segment $\overline{AB}$. Then the length of rectangle $ABCD$ is equal to ($\overline{AB}$), and its width is ($\overline{BC}$).

The area of the shaded region is equal to the area of rectangle $ABCD$ minus the area of triangle EBC.

Recall that the area of a rectangle is equal to the product of its length and its width. Thus,

Area of rectangle $ABCD = (\overline{AB})(\overline{BC})$.

The area of a triangle is equal to $\frac{1}{2}bh$. Thus,

Area of triangle $EBC = \frac{1}{2}(\overline{EB})(\overline{BC})$

But ($\overline{EB}$) $= \frac{1}{4}(\overline{BC})$. Hence

$$\text{Area of triangle } EBC = \frac{1}{2}\left(\frac{1}{4}(\overline{AB})\right)(\overline{BC})$$
$$= \frac{1}{8}(\overline{AB})(\overline{BC})$$

Since the area of triangle EBC is equal to 12 square units, we have

$$\frac{1}{8}(\overline{AB})(\overline{BC}) = 12$$

or ($\overline{AB}$)($\overline{BC}$) = 96.

But, ($\overline{AB}$)($\overline{BC}$) is the area of rectangle $ABCD$. Hence, area of rectangle $ABCD = 96$ square units.

Thus, area of shaded region equals

96 − 12 = 84 square units.

The correct answer is (C).

■ PROBLEM I.60

Suppose the average of two numbers is WX. If the first number is X, what is the other number?

(A) $WX - X$ (D) $WX - 2X$

(B) $2WX - W$ (E) $2WX - X$

(C) W

SOLUTION

(E)   The average of two numbers is obtained by adding the two numbers together and dividing by 2.

We are given that the average of two numbers is WX. We are given that X is the first number. We can let Y represent the second number in the average of the two numbers.

$$\frac{X + Y}{2} = WX$$

Solving for Y, we get

$$X + Y = 2(WX)$$

$$Y = 2WX - X$$

The correct choice is (E).

■ PROBLEM I.61

Find the slope of a line whose equation is $y = -6x + 3$.

(A) $-\dfrac{1}{6}$ (D) -6

(B) 6 (E) -3

(C) 3

SOLUTION

(D) The slope of a line in the form $y = mx + b$ is given by the coefficient of x.

If $y = -6x + 3$, we can see that the slope m is equal to -6.

The correct choice is (D).

■ PROBLEM 1.62

Solve for the value of y:
$$3x + 2y = 12$$
$$2x - 2y = 8$$

(A) 0   (D) 4

(B) 2   (E) 5

(C) 3

SOLUTION

(A) $3x + 2y = 12$

$2x - 2y = 8$

If we add these two equations together, we get

$3x + 2y = 12$

$\underline{2x - 2y = 8}$

$5x + 0 = 20$

$5x = 20$

$x = 4$

To find the value of y, we substitute 4 for x in the equation above and solve for y.

$3x + 2y = 12$

$3(4) + 2y = 12$

$12 + 2y = 12$

$2y = 0$

$y = 0$

The correct answer is (A).

■ PROBLEM I.63

One side of a rectangle is twice the length of the other side, and the perimeter is 36. Find the area of the rectangle.

(A) 48   (D) 128

(B) 72   (E) 144

(C) 90

SOLUTION

(B)   Let x = the length of the rectangle

$2x$ = the length of the other side

We are given that the perimeter of the rectangle is equal to 36.

The perimeter is equal to the sum of the length of its sides. Therefore,

$$x + 2x + x + 2x = 36$$

$$6x = 36$$

$$x = 6$$

One side of the rectangle is 6. The other side is $2x = 12$.

To obtain the area of a rectangle, we must multiply the length of one side by the length of the other side.

$$\text{Area} = x(2x) = 2x^2 = 2(6)^2 = 2(36) = 72$$

The correct choice is (B).

■ PROBLEM I.64

How long of a metal bar do you need to make a basketball hoop with a diameter of 48 cm?

(A) 75.36 cm   (D) 602.88 cm

(B) 150.72 cm   (E) 15,072 cm

(C) 301.44 cm

SOLUTION

(B)   We are interested in finding the circumference of the hoop. We are given that the diameter is 48 cm.

The circumference of a circle is found by using the equation

Circumference $= \pi d$.

The value of $\pi = 3.14$. Therefore,

Circumference $= \pi(48)$

$$= (3.14)(48)$$

$$= 150.72$$

(B) is the correct choice.

◼ PROBLEM I.65

The length of a rectangle is four more than twice the width. The perimeter of the rectangle is 44 meters. Find the length.

(A) 6 m   (D) 16 m

(B) 8 m   (E) 22 m

(C) 11 m

SOLUTION

(D)   Let $w =$ width of the rectangle

$2w + 4 =$ length of the rectangle

We are given that the perimeter of the rectangle is 44. Therefore,

Perimeter $= 2(w) + 2(l)$

$2(w) + 2(2w + 4) = 44$.

We can now solve for w.

$$2w + 4w + 8 = 44$$

$$6w + 8 = 44$$

$$6w = 36$$

$$w = 6$$

In order to find the length, we substitute 6 into the expression $2w + 4$.

$2w + 4 = 2(6) + 4 = 16$

The length is 16.

The correct choice is (D).

PROBLEM I.66

Which of the following represent functions?

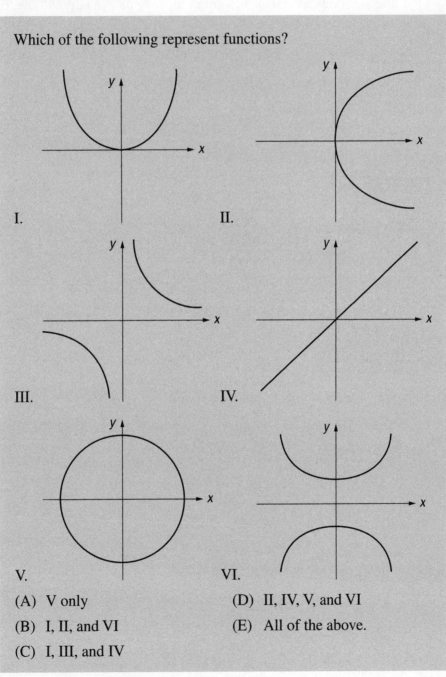

I.

II.

III.

IV.

V.

VI.

(A) V only

(B) I, II, and VI

(C) I, III, and IV

(D) II, IV, V, and VI

(E) All of the above.

SOLUTION

(C)   *Quick and easy function test to use when the graph is given to you:*

1)   Draw a vertical line through the graph.

2)   If the line you drew intersects the graph in *only one* point: *Yes*, it is a function.

   If the line you drew intersects the graph in *more than one* point: *No*, it is not a function.

I.   The line intersects the graph in *one* point.

   Yes, it is a function.

   [Parabola opening upward]

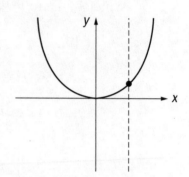

II.   The line intersects the graph in *two* points.

   No, it is not a function.

   [Parabola opening sideways]

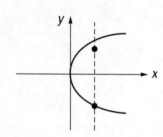

III.   The line intersects the graph in *one* point.

   Yes, it is a function

   [Hyperbola of the form $xy = c$]

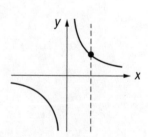

IV.   The line intersects the graph in *one* point.

   Yes, it is a function.

   [Straight line]

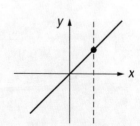

V. The line intersects the graph in *two* points.

No, it is not a function.

[Circle]

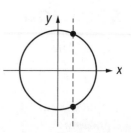

VI. The line intersects the graph in *two* points.

No, it is not a function.

[Hyperbola of the form $\dfrac{y^2}{a^2} - \dfrac{x^2}{b^2} = 1$]

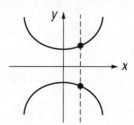

So, the correct answer is (C).

Note: When your vertical line intersects the graph in two points, this means there are *two y-values* for a given *x*-value (not a function).

To summarize:

1) *Functions*—parabolas opening up or down; hyperbolas of the form xy = c; straight lines (except vertical ones).

2) *Not functions*—parabolas opening right or left; hyperbolas of the form

$$\frac{x^2}{a^2} - \frac{y^2}{b^2} = 1, \text{ or } \frac{y^2}{a^2} - \frac{x^2}{b^2} = 1;$$

circles; ellipses.

■ PROBLEM I.67

In the figure shown below, find *x*.

(A) 50

(B) 80

(C) 120

(D) 130

(E) 150

SOLUTION

(D)   The sum of the angles of a triangle is 180°.

$$\angle A + \angle B + y = 180°$$

Since $\angle A = 60$ and $\angle B = 70$, we can substitute these values in the above equation.

$$60 + 70 + y = 180°$$

Solving for y, we find that $y = 50°$.

$\angle BCD$ is adjacent to $\angle BCA$ and forms a straight line. Therefore, $\angle BCD$ and $\angle BCA$ are supplementary. The sum of supplementary angles totals 180°.

So $x + y = 180°$

$$x + 50 = 180°$$

$$x = 130°$$

The correct choice is (D).

◼ PROBLEM I.68

Billy walked home from school 7 blocks east, 5 blocks north, 1 block west, and 3 blocks north again. How many blocks, in a straight line, is Billy's home from school?

(A) 5   (D) 16

(B) 10   (E) 20

(C) 15

SOLUTION

(B)   It is easier to visualize the straight line to Billy's house from school if we draw a diagram.

We can see that the shortest distance between Billy's home and school is the hypotenuse of a right triangle.

Since Billy walked 7 blocks east and 1 block west, he is 6 blocks east of school. Since he walked 5 blocks north and 3 blocks north, Billy is 8 blocks north of school.

Using the Pythagorean Theorem on the triangle that is formed, we find that the square of the hypotenuse equals the sum of the squares of the other two sides.

$$a^2 + b^2 = c^2$$

$$(6)^2 + (8)^2 = c^2$$

$$36 + 64 = c^2$$

$$100 = c^2$$

$$10 = c$$

(B) is the correct answer.

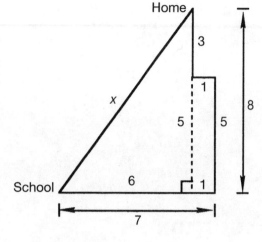

■ PROBLEM I.69

The U.S. soccer team won 70% of the games they played. If they played a total of 20 games, how many games did they lose?

(A) 6   (D) 12

(B) 8   (E) 14

(C) 10

SOLUTION

(A)   If the U.S. soccer team won 70% of the games they played, then they lost 30% of the games. Since they played a total of 20 games, we need to convert 30% to a decimal and multiply to find the number lost.

$$30\% = .30$$

$$30\% \text{ of } 20 = .30(20) = 6$$

The correct choice is (A).

■ PROBLEM I.70

Find the area of a sector of a circle with a radius of 16 cm and a 45°
arc.

(A) 6.24 cm²   (D) 803.84 cm²

(B) 100.48 cm²   (E) 2,260.8 cm²

(C) 720 cm²

SOLUTION

(B)   Radius = 16 cm

           Arc = 45°

           π = 3.14

The area of a sector equals

$$\left(\frac{\text{degrees of given arc}}{360}\right)\pi r^2.$$

Substituting the given values for the radius and arc, we have

$$\text{Area} = \left(\frac{45}{360}\right)3.14(16)^2.$$

Simplifying we get

$$\text{Area} = \frac{1}{8}(3.14)(256)$$

$$= 32(3.14)$$

$$= 100.48 \text{ cm}^2$$

The correct answer is (B).

■ PROBLEM I.71

At a certain restaurant the cost of 3 sandwiches, 7 cups of coffee, and 4 pieces of pie is $10.20, while the cost of 4 sandwiches, 8 cups of coffee, and 5 pieces of pie is $12.25. What is the cost of a luncheon consisting of one sandwich, one cup of coffee, and one piece of pie?

(A) $2.00   (D) $2.15

(B) $2.05   (E) $2.25

(C) $2.10

SOLUTION

(B)   Let x = cost of one sandwich

y = cost of one cup of coffee

z = cost of one piece of pie

So 3 sandwiches, 7 cups of coffee, and 4 pieces of pie equals $10.20 can be written as

$3x + 7y + 4z = 10.20.$

Similarly, 4 sandwiches, 8 cups of coffee, and 5 pieces of pie equal $12.25 can be written as

$4x + 8y + 5z = 12.25.$

If we subtract the two equations, we find that $x + y + z = 2.05$.

$$4x + 8y + 5z = 12.25$$
$$\underline{3x + 7y + 4z = 10.20}$$
$$x + y + z = 2.05$$

This means that the cost of one sandwich, one cup of coffee, and one piece of pie is $2.05.

The correct choice is (B).

■ PROBLEM I.72

An airplane travels 1,800 miles in 3 hours flying with the wind. On the return trip, flying against the wind it takes 4 hours to travel 2,000 miles. Find the rate of the plane in still air.

(A) 425 mph   (D) 550 mph

(B) 500 mph   (E) 600 mph

(C) 542 mph

SOLUTION

(D)   The actual speed of the plane in still air is equal to the speed of the plane minus the wind speed when going with the wind.

Likewise, the actual speed of the plane in still air is equal to the speed of the plane plus wind speed when going against the wind.

Using the formula distance = (rate) (time), we see that

$$\text{Rate} = \frac{\text{Distance}}{\text{time}}.$$

The speed (or rate) of the airplane with the wind is

$$\text{Rate} = \frac{1,800 \text{ miles}}{3 \text{ hrs}} = 600 \text{ miles/hr}.$$

So 600 mi/hr – wind speed = actual rate of airplane flying with the wind.

On the return trip, the rate of the plane is found as follows:

$$\text{Rate} = \frac{2,000 \text{ miles}}{4 \text{ hrs}} = 500 \text{ miles/hr}$$

500 miles/hr + wind speed = actual rate of airplane flying against the wind.

Travelling with the wind produces a positive wind speed while traveling against the wind produces a negative wind speed.

Let w = wind speed

x = actual speed of plane in still air

$x = 600$ miles/hr – w (with the wind)

$x = 500$ miles/hr + w (against the wind)

Setting these two equations equal, we get

600 miles/hr $- w = 500$ miles/hr $- (-w)$

600 miles/hr $- w = 500$ miles/hr $+ w$

Solving for w,

$2w = 100$ miles/hr

$w = 50$ miles/hr

Substituting $w = 50$ into either initial equation gives us a value for x.

$x = 600$ miles/hr $- 50$ miles/hr

$x = 550$ miles/hr

The correct answer is (D).

■ PROBLEM I.73

> If a triangle of base 6 units has the same area as a circle of radius 6 units, what is the altitude of the triangle?
>
> (A) π (D) 12π
>
> (B) 3π (E) 36π
>
> (C) 6π

SOLUTION

(D)   The formula for the area of a triangle is

$$A = \frac{1}{2}bh$$

where b denotes the base and h denotes the altitude.

The formula for the area of a circle is

$$A = \pi r2$$

where $\pi = 3.14$ and r denotes the radius.

Since $b = 6$, then the area of the triangle is

$$A = \frac{1}{2}(6)h = 3h.$$

We are given that the radius is 6. Substituting this value for r in the formula for the area of a circle, we obtain

$$A = \pi(6)^2 = 36\pi.$$

Since the area is the same for both figures, we can say that $3h = 36\pi$.

Solving for h, we find that

$$h = \frac{36\pi}{3} = 12\pi.$$

Therefore, the altitude of the triangle is 12π.

The correct choice is (D).

PROBLEM I.74

How many different segments are determined by 6 points on a line?

(A) 12   (D) 21

(B) 15   (E) 30

(C) 17

SOLUTION

(B)

Label the points A, B, C, D, E, and F as shown.

Then the line segments are

$\overline{AB}$				
$\overline{AC}$	$\overline{BC}$			
$\overline{AC}$	$\overline{BD}$	$\overline{CD}$		
$\overline{AE}$	$\overline{BE}$	$\overline{CE}$	$\overline{DE}$	
$\overline{AF}$	$\overline{BF}$	$\overline{CF}$	$\overline{DF}$	$\overline{EF}$
5	4	3	2	1

There are 15 segments.

The correct choice is (B).

■ PROBLEM I.75

It takes 15 apples to make 4 pies. How many pies can be made from 20 apples?

(A) 4

(D) 5

(B) $4\dfrac{1}{3}$

(E) $5\dfrac{1}{3}$

(C) $4\dfrac{2}{3}$

SOLUTION

(E)   The ratio of apples to pies is $\frac{15}{4}$.

We need to find how many pies we can make from 20 apples. So, we need to set up a proportion.

$$\frac{15}{4} = \frac{20}{x}$$

We solve for x by cross multiplying.

$$15x = 4\,(20)$$

$$15x = 80$$

$$x = \frac{80}{15}$$

$$x = 5\frac{1}{3}$$

The correct choice is (E).

■ PROBLEM I.76

Emile receives a flat weekly salary of $240 plus 12% commission of the total volume of all sales he makes. What must his dollar volume be in a week if he is to make a total weekly salary of $540?

(A) $2,800   (D) $2,500

(B) $3,600   (E) $2,000

(C) $6,400

SOLUTION

(D)   Let x = total value of all sales

$12\%x = .12x$ = Emile's commission

$240 + .12x$ = Emile's weekly salary

If Emile receives $540 one week, then

$$240 + .12x = \$540$$

$$.12x = \$300$$

$$x - \frac{\$300}{.12} = \$2,500$$

The correct choice is (D).

■ PROBLEM I.77

The area of $\triangle ADE$, an equilateral triangle, is 12 square units. If B is the midpoint of $\overline{AD}$ and C is the midpoint of $\overline{AE}$, what is the area of $\triangle ABC$?

(A) 2 square units   (D) 4 square units

(B) 3 square units   (E) 6 square units

(C) $3\frac{1}{2}$ square units

SOLUTION

(B) Let F be the midpoint of $\overline{DE}$. The four small triangles ABC, CEF, BFD, and BCF are then congruent. This means they have the same size and the same shape.

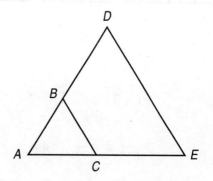

Hence, each small triangle is $\frac{1}{4}$ the area of the larger triangle $\triangle ADE$.

$$\text{area } \triangle ABC = \frac{1}{4}\text{area } \triangle ADE$$

Therefore, the area of

$$\triangle ABC = \frac{1}{4}(12) = 3.$$

The correct choice is (B).

◼ PROBLEM I.78

If $6x + 12 = 5$, then the value of $(x + 2)$ is

(A) $-\dfrac{19}{6}$.

(B) $-1\dfrac{1}{6}$.

(C) $\dfrac{5}{6}$.

(D) $3\dfrac{1}{6}$.

(E) $1\dfrac{1}{6}$.

SOLUTION

(C) We must first solve for x.

$$6x + 12 = 5$$

$$6x = -7$$

$$x = -\frac{7}{6}$$

We want the value of $(x + 2)$. Since $x = -\frac{7}{6}$, we substitute this value for x in the equation.

$$(x+2) = \left(-\frac{7}{6}\right) + 2$$

$$(x+2) = \left(-\frac{7}{6}\right) + \frac{12}{6}$$

$$x + 2 = \frac{5}{6}$$

Therefore, the correct answer is (C).

■ PROBLEM I.79

What is the value of x in the equation $\sqrt{5x - 4} - 5 = -1$?

(A) 2

(D) 4

(B) 5

(E) -4

(C) No value

SOLUTION

(D) $\sqrt{5x - 4} - 5 = -1$

The best approach to this problem would be to isolate the radical. This is accomplished by adding 5 to both sides.

$$\sqrt{5x - 4} - 5 + 5 = -1 + 5$$

$$\sqrt{5x - 4} = 4$$

We can now square both sides.

$$\left(\sqrt{5x - 4}\right)^2 = 4^2$$

$$5x - 4 = 16$$

Solving for x we obtain

$$5x - 4 + 4 = 16 + 4$$
$$5x = 20$$
$$x = \frac{20}{5}$$
$$x = 4$$

The correct answer is (D).

■ PROBLEM I.80

If R, S, and Q can wallpaper a house in 8 hours and R and S can do it in 12 hours, how long will it take Q alone to wallpaper the house?

(A) 12 hours   (D) 20 hours

(B) 24 hours   (E) 28 hours

(C) 8 hours

SOLUTION

(B)   Let x = the number of hours it takes Q to wallpaper the house by himself.

In 1 hour Q will wallpaper $\frac{1}{x}$ of the house.

Since it takes R, S, and Q eight hours to do the job if they work together, it follows that R, S, and Q complete $\frac{1}{8}$ of the house in 1 hour.

If R and S work together, they complete the job in 12 hours. Hence, in 1 hour they can complete $\frac{1}{12}$ of the house.

If all three of them work together, they can wallpaper $(\frac{1}{12} + \frac{1}{x})$ of the house in 1 hour. But we know that all three of them wallpaper $\frac{1}{8}$ of the house in 1 hour. Thus,

$$\frac{1}{x} + \frac{1}{12} = \frac{1}{8}$$

Solving this equation for x yields the number of hours it takes Q to wallpaper the house by himself.

$$\frac{1}{x} + \frac{1}{12} = \frac{1}{8}$$

$$\frac{1}{x} = \frac{1}{8} - \frac{1}{12}$$

We must simplify $\frac{1}{8} - \frac{1}{12}$ by find the lowest common denominator.

$$\frac{1}{8} = \frac{3}{24}$$

$$\frac{1}{12} = \frac{2}{24}$$

Therefore,

$$\frac{1}{x} = \frac{3}{24} - \frac{2}{24}$$

$$\frac{1}{x} = \frac{1}{24}$$

Cross multiplying we find that $x = 24$.

The correct choice is (B).

■ PROBLEM I.81

If a and b are odd integers, which of the following must be an even integer?

I. $\dfrac{a+b}{2}$

II. $ab - 1$

III. $\dfrac{ab+1}{2}$

(A) I only.

(B) II only.

(C) I and II only.

(D) II and III only.

(E) I, II, and III.

SOLUTION

(B) Let $a = 2n + 1$

$b = 2m + 1$

Take each case individually.

I. $$\frac{a+b}{2} = \frac{(2n+1)+(2m+1)}{2}$$
$$= \frac{2n+2m+2}{2}$$
$$= \frac{2(n+m+1)}{2}$$
$$= n+m+1$$

This is not necessarily even.

II. $ab - 1 = (2n + 1)(2m + 1) - 1$

$$= (4mn + 2n + 2m + 1) - 1$$

Combining the numerical terms and factoring out 2, we get

$ab - 1 = 2(2mn + m + n)$.

This will always be divisible by 2.

III. $$\frac{ab+1}{2} = \frac{(2n+1)+(2m+1)+1}{2}$$
$$= \frac{4mn+2n+2m+1+1}{2}$$
$$= 2nm + m + m + 1$$
$$= 2nm + 2m + 1$$
$$= 2(nm + m) + 1$$

This is always odd.

Hence, only II is even.

The correct choice is (B).

■ PROBLEM I.82

Which of the following equations can be used to find a number n, such that if you multiply it by 3 and subtract 2, the result is 5 times as great as if you divide the number by 3 and add 2?

(A) $3n - 2 = 5 + \dfrac{n}{3} + 2$ (D) $5(3n - 2) = \dfrac{n}{3} + 2$

(B) $3n - 2 = 5(\dfrac{n}{3} + 2)$ (E) $5n - 2 = \dfrac{n}{3} + 2$

(C) $3n - 2 = \dfrac{5n}{3} + 2$

SOLUTION

(B)   The best approach to this problem is to follow the directions given in sequence.

Let $n =$ the number

$3n =$ three times the number

$3n - 2 =$ three times the number minus 2.

$3n - 2$ is five times as great as $\dfrac{n}{3} + 2$.

$3n - 2 = 5(\dfrac{n}{3} + 2)$

The correct answer is (B).

■ PROBLEM I.83

If it takes s sacks of grain to feed c chickens, how many sacks of grain are needed to feed k chickens?

(A) $\dfrac{ck}{s}$ (D) $\dfrac{c}{sk}$

(B) $\dfrac{k}{cs}$ (E) $\dfrac{sk}{c}$

(C) $\dfrac{cs}{k}$

SOLUTION

(E)   Let s = number of sacks of grain

c = number of chickens

$\dfrac{s}{c}$ = number of sacks of grain needed to feed one chicken.

If we have k chickens, we will need to multiply the number of sacks of grain needed to feed one chicken by k. Therefore,

$$\frac{s}{c} \times k = \frac{sk}{c}$$

The answer is (E).

■ PROBLEM I.84

In the five-pointed star shown, what is the sum of the measures of angles A, B, C, D, and E?

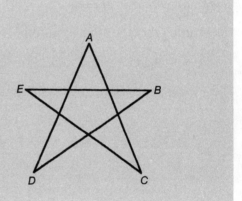

(A) 108°

(B) 72°

(C) 36°

(D) 150°

(E) 180°

SOLUTION

(E)   Let $m\angle A$ represent the measure of angle A. Though there are several ways to attack this question, one way is to recall that the sum of the measures of the three interior angles of a triangle is equal to 180°, and the measure of an exterior angle of a triangle is equal to the sum of the measures of the two non-adjacent interior angles of the triangle.

We can now start by considering triangle ACL. Of course,

$$m\angle A + m\angle C + m\angle 1 = 180°. \quad (1)$$

But $\angle 1$ is an exterior angle to triangle LEF, thus,

$$m\angle 1 = m\angle E + m\angle 2.$$

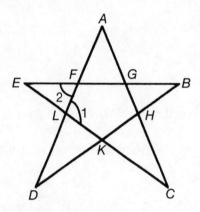

Substituting this in equation (1) yields,

$$m\angle A + m\angle C + m\angle E + m\angle 2 = 180°. \quad (2)$$

However, $\angle 2$ is an exterior angle to triangle FBD, thus,

$$m\angle 2 = m\angle B + m\angle D.$$

Substituting this result in equation (2) yields,

$$m\angle A + m\angle C + m\angle E + m\angle B + \mu\angle D = 180°.$$

Thus, the sum of the measures of angles A, B, C, D, and E is equal to $180°$.

■ PROBLEM I.85

Mary drove from Jamestown to Aberdeen, a distance of 100 miles at an average speed of 40 miles per hour. She made the return trip at an average speed of 60 miles per hour. What was her average speed for the round trip?

(A) 48 mph   (D) 51 mph

(B) 49 mph   (E) 52 mph

(C) 50 mph

SOLUTION

(A)   Distance = rate × time

$$\text{Time} = \frac{\text{Distance}}{\text{rate}}$$

Going to Aberdeen from Jamestown took

$$\frac{100 \text{ miles}}{40 \text{ miles/hr}} = \frac{5}{2} \text{ hrs.}$$

The return trip to Jamestown took

$$\frac{100 \text{ miles}}{60 \text{ miles/hr}} = \frac{5}{3} \text{ hrs.}$$

Therefore, the total time for the round trip was

$$\frac{5}{2} + \frac{5}{3} = \text{ total time}$$

In order to add these fractions, we need to find a common denominator.

$$\frac{5}{2} = \frac{15}{6}$$

$$\frac{5}{3} = \frac{10}{6}$$

$$\frac{15}{6} + \frac{10}{6} = \frac{25}{6} \text{ hours}$$

The average speed or rate for the total trip is found by dividing the total distance travelled by the total time.

$$\frac{\text{total distance (round trip)}}{\text{total time}} = \frac{100 + 100}{\left(\frac{26}{6}\right)}$$

$$= \frac{200}{\frac{25}{6}}$$

$$200 \times \frac{6}{25} = 48 \text{ miles/hr}$$

The correct answer is (A).

◼ PROBLEM I.86

Which of the following statements are true, if

$$x + y + z = 10$$

$$y \geq 5$$

$$4 \geq z \geq 3$$

I. $x < z$

II. $x > y$

III. $x + z \leq y$

(A) I only.   (D) I and III.

(B) II only.   (E) I, II, and III.

(C) III only.

SOLUTION

(D) $x + y + z = 10$

$$y \geq 5$$

$$4 \geq z \geq 3$$

Solving for x we obtain

$$x = 10 - y - z.$$

If we use the smallest values for y and z ($y = 5$ and $z = 3$), we obtain the largest value for x.

$$x = 10 - y - z$$

$$= 10 - 5 - 3$$

$$= 2$$

This implies that $x \leq 2$. Then $x < z$ and $x < y$. Consider again

$$x = 10 - y - z$$

$$x + z = 10 - y$$

Now rearrange this expression to analyze proposition III.

If $\quad y = 5$ (the smallest value),

$\quad x + z = 5$.

If $\quad y > 5$, then $x + z < 5$.

Therefore, $x + z \leq y$ making both I and III correct.

The correct choice is (D).

■ PROBLEM I.87

Which of the following equations can be used to find a woman's present age if she is now 6 times as old as her son and next year her age will be equal to the square of her son's age?

(A) $6w + 1 = w^2 + 1$ (D) $6w + 1 = (w + 1)^2$

(B) $6(w + 1) = w^2 + 1$ (E) $w + 6 = (w + 1)^2$

(C) $6(w + 1) = (w + 1)^2$

SOLUTION

(D)   Let

$\quad w = $ age of the son now

$\quad w + 1 = $ age of the son next year

$\quad 6w = $ age of the mother now

$\quad 6w + 1 = $ age of the mother next year

We are given that next year the age of the mother ($6w + 1$) will equal the square of her son's age $(w + 1)^2$.

So:

$\quad 6w + 1 = (w + 1)^2$.

The correct choice is (D).

■ PROBLEM I.88

If the length of a rectangle is increased by 30% and the width is decreased by 20%, then the area is increased by

(A) 10%.   (D) 20%.

(B) 5%.   (E) 25%.

(C) 4%.

SOLUTION

(C)   Let

$x =$ length of the rectangle

$y =$ width of the rectangle

If the length is increased by 30%, we can represent the new length by

$x + .30x = 1.3x$

If the width is decreased by 20%, we can represent the new width by

$y - .20y = .80y$

Since the area of a rectangle is found by multiplying length times width, the new area is found as follows:

new area $= (1.3x)(.80y)$

Simplifying we get

new area $= 1.04xy$

The area of the old rectangle is xy.

area new rectangle $-$ area old rectangle $=$

$1.04xy - 1.0xy = .04xy$

We can convert the coefficient .04 to a percent by multiplying by 100.

$.04 \times 100\% = 4\%$

The correct choice is (C).

■ PROBLEM I.89

What is the smallest positive number that leaves a remainder of 2 when the number is divided by 3, 4, or 5?

(A) 22   (D) 122

(B) 42   (E) 182

(C) 62

SOLUTION

(C) We must first find the least common multiple (LCM) of 3, 4, and 5. This is obtained simply by multiplying $3 \times 4 \times 5$.

$3 \times 4 \times 5 = 60$

60 is the LCM.

60 is divisible by 3.

60 is divisible by 4.

60 is divisible by 5.

In order to guarantee that the remainder in each case upon division by 3, 4, or 5 is 2, we simply add 2 to 60 to get 62.

The correct answer is (C).

■ PROBLEM I.90

If $\frac{a}{x} - \frac{b}{y} = c$ and $xy = \frac{1}{c}$, then $bx =$

(A) $1 - ay$ (D) $ay - 1$

(B) ay (E) $2ay$

(C) $ay + 1$

SOLUTION

(D) $\frac{a}{x} - \frac{b}{y} = c$ and $xy = \frac{1}{c}$

The first step would be to combine the terms on the left side of the equations over a common denominator.

$$\frac{y}{y} \times \frac{a}{x} - \frac{x}{x} \times \frac{b}{y} = c$$

$$\frac{ay - bx}{xy} = c$$

We can now simplify the expression and solve for bx.

$$\frac{ay - bx}{xy} = c$$

Multiplying both sides of the equation by xy, we obtain

$$\frac{xy(ay - bx)}{xy} = c\, xy$$

$$ay - bx = c\, xy$$

Subtracting ay from both sides and multiplying by -1, we obtain

$$bx = ay - c\, xy$$

Since we know that $xy = \frac{1}{c}$, we may substitute this value in the equation.

$$bx = ay - c\left(\frac{1}{c}\right)$$

This can be further simplified to give us the following:

$$bx = ay - 1$$

The correct choice is therefore (D).

■ PROBLEM I.91

Joe and Jim together have 14 marbles. Jim and Tim together have 10 marbles. Joe and Tim together have 12 marbles. What is the maximum number of marbles that any of these may have?

(A) 7

(B) 8

(C) 9

(D) 10

(E) 11

SOLUTION

(B)   Let

x = the number of marbles Joe owns

y = the number of marbles Jim owns

z = the number of marbles Tim owns

It is given that

$x + y = 14$ (1)

$y + z = 10$ (2)

$x + z = 12$ (3)

Solving for y in equation (2) we find

$y + z = 10$

$y = 10 - z$

Solving for x in equation (3) we find

$x + z = 12$

$x = 12 - z$

x and y can now be written in terms of a common variable, z. We can now substitute these terms in equation (1) to obtain

$$x + y = 14 \qquad (1)$$

$$(12 - z) + (10 - z) = 14$$

$$22 - 2z = 14$$

$$22 = 14 + 2z$$

$$22 - 14 = 2z$$

$$8 = 2z$$

$$4 = z$$

∴ We now know that Tim owns 4 marbles.

Since $x = 12 - z$, we can substitute 4 for the value of z to obtain the number of marbles owned by Joe.

$$x = 12 - z = 12 - 4 = 8$$

$\therefore$ Joe owns 8 marbles.

Likewise, since $y = 10 - z$, we can find the number of marbles owned by Jim.

$$y = 10 - z = 10 - 4 = 6$$

$\therefore$ Jim owns 6 marbles.

Joe's marbles, 8, is the maximum number of marbles anyone can have.

The correct choice is (B).

■ PROBLEM I.92

In the ABC Auto Factory, robots assemble cars. If 3 robots assemble 17 cars in 10 minutes, how many cars can 14 robots assemble in 45 minutes if all robots work at the same rate all the time?

(A) 357

(D) 150

(B) 340

(E) 272

(C) 705

SOLUTION

(A)   If 3 robots can assemble 17 cars in 10 minutes, then 3 robots can assemble $\frac{17}{10}$ cars in 1 minute. To find the number of cars that 1 robot can assemble in 1 minute, we divide $\frac{17}{10}$ by 3.

One robot assembles

$$\frac{1}{3}\left(\frac{17}{10}\right) \text{ or } \frac{17}{30}$$

of a car in 1 minute.

Similarly, if 14 robots assemble x cars in 45 minutes, then the 14 robots assemble $\frac{x}{45}$ cars in 1 minute.

Thus, 1 robot assembles

$$\frac{1}{14}\left(\frac{x}{45}\right) \text{ or } \frac{x}{14(45)}$$

of a car in 1 minute.

Since the robots all work at the same rate, we can say that

$$\frac{x}{14(45)} = \frac{17}{30}$$

$$\frac{x}{360} = \frac{17}{30}$$

Cross multiplying we get

$$30x = 17(630)$$

$$30x = 10{,}710$$

Dividing both sides of the equation by 30, we get

$$\frac{30x}{30} = \frac{10{,}710}{30}$$

$$x = 357$$

The correct choice is (A).

■ PROBLEM I.93

A postal truck leaves its station and heads for Chicago, averaging 40 mph. An error in the mailing schedule is spotted and 24 minutes after the truck leaves, a car is sent to overtake the truck. If the car averages 50 mph, how long will it take to catch the postal truck?

(A) 2.6 hours   (D) 1.5 hours

(B) 3 hours   (E) 1.6 hours

(C) 2 hours

SOLUTION

(E)   Let t = time in hours it takes the car to catch up with the postal truck

$$\left(t + \frac{24}{60}\right) = \text{time of travel of the truck}$$

$(t + .4) = $ time of travel in hours of the truck

For the truck:

     Distance = rate × time

$$D = 40\,(t + .4)$$

$$D = 40t + 16$$

For the car:

Distance = rate × time

$$D = 50 \times t$$

$$D = 50t$$

Since the distance travelled by the truck and the car are equal, we can set these two equations equal to each other to get

$$50t = 40t + 16.$$

Solving for t we get

$$50t - 40t = 16$$

$$10t = 16$$

$$t = 1.6$$

Therefore, it takes the car 1.6 hrs to catch up with the postal truck.

The correct choice is (E).

■ PROBLEM I.94

A table tennis tournament is to be round-robin; that is, each player plays one match against every other player. The winner of the tournament is determined by the best scores in the matches. How many matches will be played if 5 people enter the tournament?

(A) 10

(B) 15

(C) 20

(D) 105

(E) 120

SOLUTION

(A)   Label the players 1 through 5. Player 1 will have one match with each of the remaining 4 players. Player 2 (who has already played Player 1) will have matches with the remaining three players and so on. The total number of matches will be

$$4 + 3 + 2 + 1 = 10.$$

The correct choice is (A).

▪ PROBLEM I.95

The most economical price among the following prices is

(A) 10 oz. for 16¢.   (D) 20 oz. for 34¢.

(B) 2 oz. for 3¢.   (E) 8 oz. for 13¢.

(C) 4 oz. for 7¢.

SOLUTION

(B)   To find the most economical price we must find out what 1 oz. would cost. To do this we simply divide the price by the number of ounces.

(A)   10 oz. for 16¢ gives us 1 oz. for $\frac{16}{10} = 1.6$¢

(B)   2 oz. for 3¢ gives us 1 oz. for $\frac{3}{2} = 1.5$¢

(C)   4 oz. for 7¢ gives us 1 oz. for $\frac{7}{4} = 1.75$¢

(D)   20 oz. for 34¢ gives us 1 oz. for $\frac{34}{20} = 1.70$¢

(E)   8 oz. for 13¢ gives us 1 oz. for $\frac{13}{8} = 1.63$¢

The most economical value is therefore (B)

▪ PROBLEM I.96

Pipe 1 can fill a tank in 3 hours. Pipe 2 can fill the same tank in 5 hours. To the nearest hour, how long would it take both pipes working together to fill the tank?

(A) 1   (D) 4

(B) 2   (E) 5

(C) 3

SOLUTION

(B)   Let x = the number of hours it would take both pipes working together to fill the tank.

Pipe 1 will fill $\frac{1}{3}$ of the tank in 1 hr.

Pipe 2 will fill $\frac{1}{5}$ of the tank in 1 hr.

In x hours Pipe 1 will fill $\frac{x}{3}$ of the tank and Pipe 2 will fill $\frac{x}{5}$ tank.

Adding these two amounts together we have a full tank

$$\frac{x}{3}+\frac{x}{5}=1$$

$$\frac{5x}{5\times3}+\frac{3x}{3\times5}=1$$

$$\frac{8x}{15}=1$$

$$8x=15$$

$$x=\frac{15}{8}=1\frac{7}{8}\text{ hrs}$$

To the nearest hour this is 2.

The correct choice is (B).

PROBLEM I.97

A square is cut from a circle as shown in the diagram. If the radius of the circle is 6, what is the total area of the shaded regions?

(A) $9\pi-18$

(B) $12\pi-18$

(C) $12\pi-72$

(D) $36\pi-36$

(E) $36\pi-72$

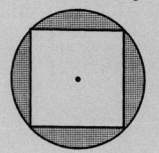

SOLUTION

(E)   Area of shaded region = area of circle – area of square

The area of the circle is $\pi(\text{radius})^2 = \pi(6)^2 = 36\pi$

The area of a square is $(\text{side})^2$.

Consider $\frac{1}{4}$ of the square where the side of the square is equal to the hypotenuse of the triangle. The legs of the triangle are then radii of the circle.

The area of the triangle is

$$\frac{1}{2}bh = \frac{1}{2}(6)(6) = 18.$$

Since we have four such triangles making up the square, the area of the square is $4 \times 18 = 72$.

The area of the shaded region is therefore $36\pi - 72$.

The correct choice is (E).

PROBLEM I.98

For non-zero numbers, p, q, r, and s, $\frac{p}{q} = \frac{r}{s}$. Which of the following statements is true?

(A) $\dfrac{p+q}{p} = \dfrac{r+s}{r}$

(D) $\dfrac{p-q}{q} = \dfrac{s-r}{r}$

(B) $\dfrac{p}{r} = \dfrac{q}{r}$

(E) $\dfrac{q}{p-q} = \dfrac{r}{s-r}$

(C) $\dfrac{r}{s} = \dfrac{q}{r}$

SOLUTION

(A) p, q, r, and s are non-zero numbers.

$$\frac{p}{q} = \frac{r}{s}$$

If we cross multiply, we see that

$$ps = qr \quad (1)$$

In answer choice (A), we see that

$$\frac{p+q}{p} = \frac{r+s}{r}$$

Cross multiplying will give us

$$r(p + q) = p(r + s)$$

Using the distribution law, we get

$$rp + rq = pr + ps$$

Since rp and pr are equal, we can rewrite the equation as follows:

$$rp + rq = rp + ps$$

Subtracting rp from both sides, we get

$$rp + rq - rp = rp + ps - rp$$

$$rq = ps$$

Since $rq = qr$, then $qr = ps$. Thus, choice (A), when rearranged, is the same as equation (1), which is known to be true.

Therefore, choice (A) is correct.

■ PROBLEM I.99

Each of the integers h, m, and n is divisible by 3. Which of the following integers is always divisible by 9?

I. hm
II. $h + m$
III. $h + m + n$

(A) I only.   (D) II and III only.

(B) II only.   (E) I, II, and III.

(C) III only.

SOLUTION

(A) h, m, and n are divisible by 3.

Let $h = 3x$

       $m = 3y$

$$n = 3z$$

I. $hm = (3x)(3y) = 9xy$

This is divisible by 9.

II. $h + m = 3x + 3y = 3(x + y)$

This is not necessarily divisible by 9.

III. $h + m + n = 3x + 3y + 3z$

$$= 3(x + y + z)$$

This is not necessarily divisible by 9.

So, the correct choice is (A).

■ PROBLEM I.100

In the figure, if $\angle AOB = 60°$ and O is the center of the circle with radius $= 6$, then the area of the shaded region is

(A) 6π

(B) $6\pi - 2$

(C) $6\pi - 4$

(D) $6\pi - 6$

(E) $6\pi - 9$

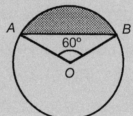

SOLUTION

(E) $\overline{OA}$ and $\overline{OB}$ are radii of the circle.

We are given that the radius is 6.

Since $\overline{OA} = \overline{OB}$, then $\angle OAB = \angle OBA$.

Since the sum of the angles of a triangle is equal to $180°$, then

$$\angle OAB + \angle OBA + \angle AOB = 180°$$

Since $\angle OAB = \angle OBA$, we can substitute $\angle OAB$ in place of $\angle OBA$. We also know that $\angle AOB$ is equal to $60°$. Therefore

$$\angle OAB + \angle OAB + 60° = 180°$$

$$2 \angle OAB + 60° = 180°$$

$$2 \angle OAB = 120°$$

$$\angle OAB = 60°$$

Since $\angle OAB = \angle OBA$, then we can say that $\angle OBA$ is also 60°. Therefore $\triangle AOB$ is equilateral and then must equal 6.

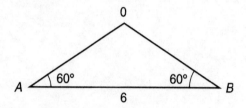

We must find the area of the triangle. The area of the triangle is $\frac{1}{2} bh$. We need to compute h by using the Pythagorean Theorem.

$$a^2 + h^2 = c^2$$
$$3^2 + h^2 = 6^2$$
$$h^2 = 36 - 9 = 27$$
$$h = \sqrt{27} = \sqrt{9} \times \sqrt{3} = 3\sqrt{3}$$

Therefore, the area of triangle $AOB = \frac{1}{2}$ (base) (height):

$$\frac{1}{2} \times 6 \times 3\sqrt{3} = 9\sqrt{3}$$

The area of sector AOB equals

$$\left(\frac{60}{360} \right) \pi(r^2) = \frac{1}{6} \pi(6)^2$$

$$= \frac{1}{6} \pi \times 36$$

$$= 6\pi$$

Finally, we can compute the area of the shaded region as follows:

Area of shaded region = area of sector AOB – area of triangle AOB.

Substituting our values for the area of sector AOB and the area of triangle AOB, we obtain

Area of shaded region = $6\pi - 9\sqrt{3}$

The correct choice is (E).

■ PROBLEM I.101

Some integers in set A are odd.
If the statement above is true, which of the following must also be true?

(A) If an integer is odd, it is in set A.

(B) If an integer is even, it is in set A.

(C) Not all integers in set A are even.

(D) All integers in set A are even.

(E) All integers in set A are odd.

SOLUTION

(C)   If some of the integers in set A are odd, then not all of the integers in set A are even. Therefore, the correct answer is (C).

■ PROBLEM I.102

If $5 < \frac{5x-6}{3} < 6$ and x is an integer, what is the value of $7x$?

(A) 2   (D) 24

(B) 8   (E) 28

(C) 16

SOLUTION

(E)   Multiply each part of the equation by 3: $15 < 5x - 6 < 18$. Add 6 to each part : $21 < 5x < 24$. Now, divide by 5: $4.2 < x < 4.8$. Since x is an integer, x must be 4. Therefore, $x = 4$ and $7x = 28$. Therefore, the correct answer is (E).

▪ PROBLEM I.103

Six different cereals, identified by T, U, V, W, X, and Y, were tested for nutritional value and cost. The results are shown below. Which brand costs more than V but also has higher nutritional value than V?

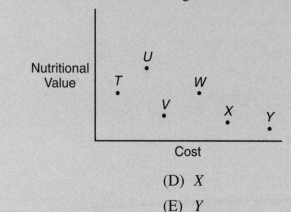

(A) T (D) X

(B) U (E) Y

(C) W

SOLUTION

(C)   The required point must lie higher on the vertical axis than V and further to the right on the horizontal axis than V. W is the only point that satisfies these requirements. The correct answer is (C).

▪ PROBLEM I.104

Squaring the product of x and 7 results in the same value as that obtained by squaring the sum of x and 11. Which of the following equations could be used to find all possible values of x?

(A) $(7 + x)^2 = (11x)^2$ (D) $(7x)^2 = (11x)^2$

(B) $(7x)^2 = (x + 11)^2$ (E) $(7 + x)^2 = (x + 11)^2$

(C) $7(11)^2 = (2x)^2$

SOLUTION

(B)   Squaring the product of x and 7 simply means to multiply x and 7, then square the result: $(7x)^2$. Squaring the sum of x and 11 means to add x to 11, then square the result: $(x + 11)^2$. To create an equation that could be used to find all possible values of x, use the fact that the results of these two processes will be equal: $(7x)^2 = (x + 11)^2$. Therefore, the correct answer is (B).

■ PROBLEM I.105

The rectangle *PRST* shown below represents a dartboard. $QR = (\frac{1}{3})(PQ)$. If a dart is thrown and lands on the dartboard, what is the probability that it lands in the shaded area?

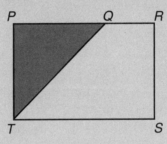

(A) $\dfrac{1}{4}$ (D) $\dfrac{5}{8}$

(B) $\dfrac{1}{3}$ (E) $\dfrac{2}{3}$

(C) $\dfrac{3}{8}$

SOLUTION

(C)   For simplicity, let $QR = 2$, so that $PQ = 6$ and $PR = 8$. Also, let $PT = 4$. The area of rectangle $PRST = (PR)(PT) = (8)(3) = 24$, whereas the area of $\triangle PQT = (\frac{1}{2})(PQ)(PT) = (\frac{1}{2})(6)(3) = 9$. The required probability $= \frac{9}{24} = \frac{3}{8}$. Therefore, the correct answer is (C).

■ PROBLEM I.106

If $X = \{5, 7, 9, 15, 16\}$ and $X \cap Y = \{9, 16\}$, which of the following sets could represent Y?

(A) $\{4, 8, 9, 16, 18\}$ (D) $\{9, 15, 16\}$

(B) $\{5, 7, 15\}$ (E) $\{5, 7, 8, 9, 12\}$

(C) $\{3, 9, 10, 15, 20\}$

SOLUTION

(A)   If $Y = \{4, 8, 9, 16, 18\}$, the common elements to X and Y, represented by $X \cap Y$, are 9 and 16. The intersections for (B), (C), (D), and (E) are as follows: $\{5, 7, 15\}$, $\{9, 15\}$, $\{9, 15, 16\}$, and $\{5, 7, 9\}$ respectively. Therefore, the correct answer is (A).

■ PROBLEM I.107

The sum of four consecutive even integers is –52. What is the sum of the squares of the largest and smallest of these integers?

(A) 169   (D) 1352

(B) 356   (E) 2704

(C) 696

SOLUTION

(B)   Let $x, x + 2, x + 4$, and $x + 6$ represent the four consecutive even integers. Then $x + (x + 2) + (x + 4) + (x + 6) = -52$. Simplifying, we get $4x + 12 = -52$, $4x = -64$, so $x = -16$. The four numbers are $-16, -14, -12$, and -10. Since the largest is -10 and the smallest is -16, we calculate: $(-10)^2 + (-16)^2 = 356$. The correct answer is (B).

■ PROBLEM I.108

The sum of four consecutive integers that are divisible by 4 is –72. What is the smallest of these integers?

(A) –12   (D) –24

(B) –16   (E) –28

(C) –20

SOLUTION

(D)   If m is the first of the given integers, then we can represent the given integers with m, $m + 4$, $m + 8$, and $m + 12$. The sum of these integers is $4m + 244 = 4(m + 6)$. Thus, $4(m + 6) = -72$, or $m = -24$. The other three integers are -20, -16, and -12. The smallest one is -24. The correct answer is (D).

■ PROBLEM I.109

An inheritance of $200,000 is split among Julia, Kay, and Laura in the ratio of 2:5:9. If Julia gets the largest share and Laura gets the smallest share, how much money does Kay receive?

(A) $112,500   (D) $25,000

(B) $85,000   (E) $12,500

(C) $62,500

SOLUTION

(C)   Let $2x =$ Laura's amount, $5x =$ Kay's amount, and $9x =$ Julia's amount. Then $2x + 5x + 9x = \$200,000$. This simplifies to $16x = \$200,000$, so $x = \$12,500$. Kay's amount $= (5)(\$12,500) = \$62,500$. The correct answer is (C).

■ PROBLEM I.110

If the graph of the equation $kx - 3y = 6$ has a slope of -12, what is the value of $-k$?

(A) -36 (D) -4

(B) -18 (E) -2

(C) -9

SOLUTION

(A)   Rewrite the equation as $-3y = -kx + 6$, which leads to $y = \frac{k}{3}(x) - 2$. The slope of -12 is identified by $\frac{k}{3}$, the coefficient of x. So, $\frac{k}{3} = -12$. Thus, $k = -36$. The correct answer is (A).

■ PROBLEM I.111

Two dice are rolled together. What is the probability of getting two numbers such that their sum is an odd integer?

(A) $\dfrac{8}{21}$ (D) $\dfrac{4}{7}$

(B) $\dfrac{5}{21}$ (E) $\dfrac{1}{3}$

(C) $\dfrac{3}{7}$

SOLUTION

(C)   There are 21 different possible incomes for this event. Among them, 9 outcomes result in two integers whose sum is an odd integer. Therefore, the required probability is $\frac{9}{21} = \frac{3}{7}$. The correct answer is (C).

■ PROBLEM I.112

Based on the scatter plot shown below, which of the following is the most logical conclusion?

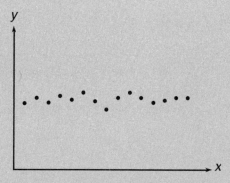

(A) As x decreases, y decreases.

(B) As x decreases, y increases.

(C) As x remains constant, y decreases.

(D) As x remains constant, y increases.

(E) As x increases, y remains constant.

SOLUTION

(E)   For the 15 points shown, it appears that as x changes, in general, y remains constant. The correct answer is (E).

■ PROBLEM I.113

What is the range of the function $f(x) = 5(x - 3) - 7$?

(A) All numbers less than or equal to 3

(B) All numbers greater than or equal to –3

(C) All numbers less than or equal to 7

(D) All numbers greater than or equal to –7

(E) All numbers between –7 and –3, inclusive

SOLUTION

(D)   This is a quadratic function whose vertex is (3, –7). Since the coefficient of x^2, namely 5, is positive, this point must be the lowest point on the graph. Thus, the range (*y* values) must be at least equal to –7. The correct answer is (D).

 PROBLEM I.114

For the number line shown below, suppose that the distance between point *J* (not shown) and *G* is the same as the distance between *G* and *H*. What coordinate is associated with point *J*?

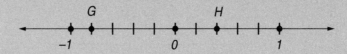

(A) $-\dfrac{11}{5}$ (D) $\dfrac{5}{6}$

(B) –2   (E) $\dfrac{6}{5}$

(C) $-\dfrac{5}{6}$

SOLUTION

(B)   The distance between *G* and *H* is $\frac{6}{5}$. Point *J* must lie $\frac{6}{5}$ units to the left of point *G*. The coordinate for *J* is found by subtracting $\frac{6}{5}$ from $-\frac{4}{5}$ to get $-\frac{10}{5}$ = –2. The correct answer is (B).

PROBLEM I.115

The pie graph shown below illustrates the percent of expenditures for a typical college student who lives in an apartment. The amount spent on books is twice the amount spent on entertainment. If the total amount spent annually is $18,000, how much is spent on books, clothing, and rent combined?

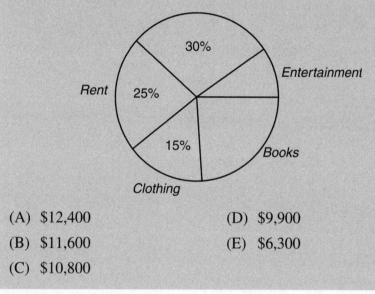

(A) $12,400   (D) $9,900

(B) $11,600   (E) $6,300

(C) $10,800

SOLUTION

(C)   The combined percent of books and entertainment is $100 - 30 - 25 - 15 = 30\%$. Since the amount spent on books is twice that spent on entertainment, 20% represents the books percentage and 10% represents the entertainment percentage. So books, clothing, and rent combined is $20 + 15 + 25 = 60\%$. Now, $(.60)(\$18,000) = \$10,800$. The correct answer is (C).

PROBLEM I.116

If $4^m = 8^{3t+1}$, which of the following is equivalent to m?

(A) $\dfrac{t+4}{1}$

(D) $\dfrac{9t+3}{2}$

(B) $\dfrac{3t+1}{2}$

(E) $\dfrac{9t+6}{2}$

(C) $\dfrac{6t+3}{5}$

SOLUTION

(D) $4^m = (2^2)^m = 2^{2m}$, $8^{3t+1} = (2^3)^{3t+1} = 2^{9t+3}$. Equating exponents, we get $2m = 9t + 3$, so $m = \frac{9t+3}{2}$. The correct answer is (D).

PROBLEM I.117

The above table shows the number of XQ games sold at different prices. Salesperson A sold one-half the total number of games priced at $100 apiece and one-half the total number of games priced at $50 apiece. Salesperson B sold only the XQ games priced at $76 apiece. If the amount of sales for these two salespeople was equal, how many XQ games did salesperson B sell?

Price of Game XQ	Total Number of Games Sold
$100	900
$76	1300
$50	2000

(A) 1,290

(D) 1,230

(B) 1,270

(E) 1,200

(C) 1,250

SOLUTION

(C) The total amount of sales for salesperson A is $(450)(\$100) + (1,000)(\$50) = \$95,000$. Since salesperson B also made \$95,000 worth of sales for the games priced at \$76 apiece, the number of games he sold is $\$95,000/\$76 = 1,250$. The correct answer is (C).

■ PROBLEM I.118

Given two different sets A and B, where $A \cup B = A$, and neither A nor B is the empty set, which of the following conclusions is valid?

(A) $A \cap B$ is the empty set   (D) B is a subset of A

(B) A is a subset of B (E) $A \cup B = B$

(C) The complement of A equals the complement of B

SOLUTION

(D) Since $A \cup B = A$, each element of B must be contained in A. Thus, B is a subset of A. For example, if $A = \{1, 2, 3, 4, 5\}$ and $B = \{3, 4, 5\}$, then $A \cup B = A$. The correct answer is (D).

■ PROBLEM I.119

If p is a prime number greater than 5, which of the following cannot be a factor of $10p^2$?

(A) p^2 (D) $7p$

(B) $2p^2$ (E) 13

(C) $5p^2$

SOLUTION

(A) $10p^2$ contains the prime factors of only 2, 5, and p. The term p^3 cannot be a factor of $10p^2$, because $\frac{10p^2}{p^3} = \frac{10}{p}$, which is not an integer. If it were, then p would necessarily be a factor of 10, which is impossible. Choices (B) and (C) are automatically factors of $10p^2$, since they can divide algebraically into $10p^2$. Choice (D) would be a factor of $10p^2$ if $p = 7$. Choice (E) would be a factor of $10p^2$ if $p = 13$. The correct answer is (A).

PROBLEM I.120

The graph of a quadratic function has two x-intercepts, -5 and 3. Which of the following points could be the vertex of this graph?

(A) $(-1, 1)$ (D) $(-4, 6)$

(B) $(-2, 3)$ (E) $(-5, 8)$

(C) $(-3, 4)$

SOLUTION

(A)   For the graph of any quadratic function with two x-intercepts, the x value of the vertex must be the average of the x values of the two x-intercepts. So x value of the vertex for this example must be $\frac{(-5+3)}{2} = -1$. Only choice (A) meets this requirement. The correct answer is (A).

PART II

STUDENT-PRODUCED RESPONSE

The Student-Produced Response format of the SAT is designed to give the student a certain amount of flexibility in answering questions. In this section the student must calculate the answer to a given question and then enter the solution into a grid. The grid is constructed so that a solution can be given in either decimal or fraction form. Either form is acceptable unless otherwise stated.

The problems in the Student-Produced Response section try to reflect situations arising in the real world. Here calculations will involve objects occurring in everyday life. There is also an emphasis on problems involving data interpretation. In keeping with this emphasis, students will be allowed the use of a calculator during the exam.

Through this review, you will learn how to successfully attack Student-Produced Response questions. Familiarity with the test format combined with solid math strategies will prove invaluable in answering the questions quickly and accurately.

ABOUT THE DIRECTIONS

Each Student-Produced Response question will require you to solve the problem and enter your answer in a grid. There are specific rules you will need to know for entering your solution. If you enter your answer in an incorrect form, you will not receive credit, even if you originally solved the problem correctly. Therefore, you should carefully study the following rules now, so you don't have to waste valuable time during the actual test:

125

For each of the questions below, solve the problem and indicate your answer by marking the ovals in the special grid, as shown in the examples below.

Answer: $\frac{9}{5}$ or 9/5 or 1.8

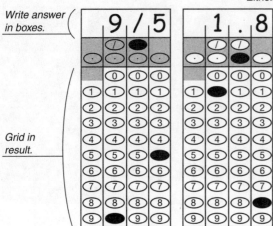

Either position correct.

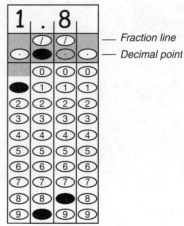

- Mark no more than one oval in any column.

- Because the answer sheet will be machine scored, you will receive credit only if the ovals are filled in correctly.

- Although not required, it is suggested that you write your answer in the boxes at the top of the columns to help you fill in the ovals accurately.

- Some problems may have more than one correct answer. In such cases, grid only one answer.

- No question has a negative answer.

- Mixed numbers such as $3\frac{1}{2}$ must be gridded as 3.5 or 7/2.

(If 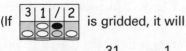 is gridded, it will be interpreted as $\frac{31}{2}$, not $3\frac{1}{2}$.)

NOTE: You may start your answers in any column, space permitting. Columns not needed should be left blank.

- **Decimal Accuracy:** If you obtain a decimal answer, enter the most accurate value the grid will accommodate. For example, if you obtain an answer such as 0.6666 ..., you should record the result as .666 or .667. Less accurate values such as .66 or .67 are not acceptable.

Acceptable ways to grid $\frac{2}{3} = .6666...$

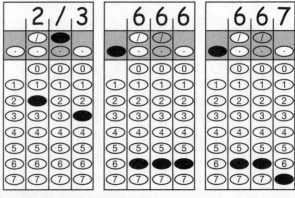

SAMPLE QUESTION

How many pounds of apples can be bought with $5.00 if apples cost $.40 a pound?

SOLUTION

Converting dollars to cents we obtain the equation

$$x = 500 \div 40$$

$$x = 12.5$$

The solution to this problem would be gridded as

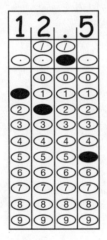

ABOUT THE QUESTIONS

Within the SAT Student-Produced Response section you will be given 10 questions. You will have 20 minutes to answer these questions. Therefore, you should work quickly.

The Student-Produced Response questions will come from the areas of numbers and operations, algebra and functions, geometry and measurement, and data analysis. There is an emphasis on word problems and on data interpretation, which usually involves reading tables to answer questions. Many of the geometry questions will refer to diagrams or will ask you to create a figure from information given in the question.

The following will detail the different types of questions you should expect to encounter on the Student-Produced Response section.

NUMBER AND OPERATION QUESTIONS

These questions test your ability to perform standard manipulations and simplifications of arithmetic expressions. For some questions, there is more than one approach. There are six kinds of arithmetic questions you may encounter in the Student-Produced Response section. For each type of question, we will show how to solve the problem and grid your answer.

Question Type 1: Properties of a Whole Number *N*

This problem tests your ability to find a whole number with a given set of properties. You will be given a list of properties of a whole number and asked to find that number.

PROBLEM

> The properties of a whole number N are
>
> (A) N is a perfect square.
>
> (B) N is divisible by 2.
>
> (C) N is divisible by 3.
>
> Grid in the second smallest whole number with the above properties.

SOLUTION

Try to first obtain the smallest number with the above properties. The smallest number with properties (B) and (C) is 6. Since property (A) says the number must be a perfect square, the smallest number with properties (A), (B), and (C) is 36.

$6^2 = 36$ is the smallest whole number with the above properties. The second smallest whole number (the solution) is

$$2^2 6^2 = 144.$$

The correct answer entered into the grid is

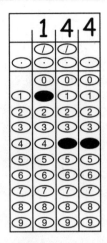

Question Type 2: Simplifying Fractions

This type of question requires you to simplify fractional expressions and grid the answer in the format specified. By canceling out terms common to both the numerator and denominator, we can simplify complex fractional expressions.

PROBLEM

Change $\dfrac{1}{2} \times \dfrac{3}{7} \times \dfrac{2}{8} \times \dfrac{14}{10} \times \dfrac{1}{3}$ to decimal form.

SOLUTION

The point here is to cancel out terms common to both the numerator and denominator. Once the fraction is brought down to lowest terms, the result is entered into the grid as a decimal.

After cancellation we are left with the fraction $\frac{1}{40}$. Equivalently,

$$\frac{1}{40} = \frac{1}{10} \times \frac{1}{4} = \frac{1}{10}(.25) = .025.$$

Hence, in our grid we enter

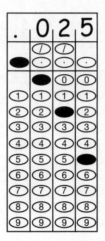

Note: If "decimal" was not specified, any correct version of the answer could be entered into the grid.

Question Type 3: Prime Numbers of a Particular Form

Here, you will be asked to find a prime number with certain characteristics. Remember—a prime number is a number that can only be divided by itself and 1.

PROBLEM

Find a prime number of the form $7k + 1 < 50$.

SOLUTION

This is simply a counting problem. The key is to list all the numbers of the form $7k + 1$ starting with $k = 0$. The first one that is prime is the solution to the problem.

The whole numbers of the form $7k + 1$ that are less than 50 are 1, 8, 15, 22, 29, 36, and 43. Of these, 29 and 43 are prime numbers. The possible solutions are 29 and 43.

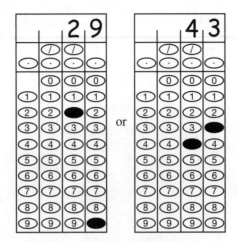

Question Type 4: Order of Operations

The following question type tests your knowledge of the arithmetic order of operations. Always work within the parentheses or with absolute values first, while keeping in mind that multiplication and division are carried out before addition and subtraction.

PROBLEM

Find a solution to the equation $x \div 3 \times 4 \div 2 = 6$.

SOLUTION

The key here is to recall the order of precedence for arithmetic operations. After simplifying the expression one can solve for x.

Since multiplication and division have the same level of precedence, we simplify the equation from left to right to obtain

$$\frac{x}{3} \times 4 \div 2 = 6$$

$$\frac{4x}{3} \div 2 = 6$$

$$\frac{2x}{3} = 6$$

$$x = 9$$

As 9 solves the above problem, our entry in the grid is

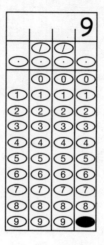

Question Type 5: Solving for Ratios

This type of question tests your ability to manipulate ratios given a set of constraints.

PROBLEM

Let A, B, C, and D be positive integers. Assume that the ratio of A to B is equal to the ratio of C to D. Find a possible value for A if the product of $BC = 24$ and D is odd.

SOLUTION

The quickest way to find a solution is to list the possible factorizations of 24:

1×24

2×12

3×8

4×6

Since $AD = BC = 24$ and D is odd, the only possible solution is $A = 8$ (corresponding to $D = 3$).

In the following grid we enter

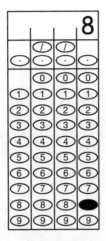

Question Type 6: Simplifying Arithmetic Expressions

Here you will be given an arithmetic problem that is easier to solve if you transform it into a basic algebra problem. This strategy saves valuable time by cutting down on the number and complexity of computations involved.

PROBLEM

Simplify $1 - \left(\dfrac{1}{2} + \dfrac{1}{4} + \dfrac{1}{8} + \dfrac{1}{16} + \dfrac{1}{32} + \dfrac{1}{64} \right)$.

SOLUTION

This problem can be done one of two ways. The "brute force" approach would be to get a common denominator and simplify. An approach involving less computation is given below.

Set $S = 1 - \left(\dfrac{1}{2} + \dfrac{1}{4} + \dfrac{1}{8} + \dfrac{1}{16} + \dfrac{1}{32} + \dfrac{1}{64} \right)$

Multiplying this equation by 2 we obtain

$$2S = 2 - \left(1 + \frac{1}{2} + \frac{1}{4} + \frac{1}{8} + \frac{1}{16} + \frac{1}{32}\right)$$

$$2S = 1 - \left(\frac{1}{2} + \frac{1}{4} + \frac{1}{8} + \frac{1}{16} + \frac{1}{32}\right)$$

$$2S = 1 - \left(\frac{1}{2} + \frac{1}{4} + \frac{1}{8} + \frac{1}{16} + \frac{1}{32} + \frac{1}{64}\right) + \frac{1}{64}$$

$$2S = S + \frac{1}{64}$$

$$S = \frac{1}{64}$$

We enter into the grid

ALGEBRA AND FUNCTION QUESTIONS

Within the Student-Produced Response section, you will also encounter algebra questions that will test your ability to solve algebraic expressions in the setting of word problems. You may encounter the following six types of algebra questions during the SAT. As in the previous section, we provide methods for approaching each type of problem.

Question Type 1: Solving a System of Linear Equations

This is a standard question that will ask you to find the solution to a system of two linear equations with two unknowns.

PROBLEM

Consider the system of simultaneous equations given by

$$y - 2 = x - 4$$
$$y + 3 = 6 - x$$

Solve for the quantity $6y + 3$.

SOLUTION

This problem can be solved by taking the first equation given and solving for x. This would yield

$$x = y + 2.$$

Next, we plug this value for x into the second equation, giving us

$$y + 3 = 6 - (y + 2).$$

Solve this equation for y and we get

$$y = \frac{1}{2}.$$

We are asked to solve for $6y + 3$, so we can plug our value for y in and get

$$6(\tfrac{1}{2}) + 3 = 6.$$

Our answer is 6 and gridded correctly it is

Question Type 2: Word Problems Involving Age

When dealing with this type of question, you will be asked to solve for the age of a particular person. The question may require you to determine how much older one person is, how much younger one person is, or the specific age of the person.

PROBLEM

> Tim is 2 years older than Jane and Joe is 4 years younger than Jane. If the sum of the ages of Jane, Joe, and Tim is 28, how old is Joe?

SOLUTION

Define Jane's age to be the variable x and work from there.

Let

Jane's age $= x$

Tim's age $= x + 2$

Joe's age $= x - 4$

Summing up the ages we get

$$x + x + 2 + x - 4 = 28$$

$$3x - 2 = 28$$

$$3x = 30$$

$$x = 10$$

Joe's age $= 10 - 4 = 6$.

Hence, we enter into the grid

Question Type 3: Word Problems Involving Money

Word problems involving money will test your ability to translate the information given into an algebraic statement. You will also be required to solve your algebraic statement.

PROBLEM

After receiving his weekly paycheck on Friday, a man buys a television for $100, a suit for $200, and a radio for $50. If the total money he spent amounts to 40% of his paycheck, what is his weekly salary?

SOLUTION

Simply set up an equation involving the man's expenditures and the percentage of his paycheck that he used to buy them.

Let the amount of the man's paycheck equal x. We then have the equation

$$40\%x = 100 + 200 + 50$$

$$0.4x = 350$$

$$x = \$875$$

In the grid we enter

Question Type 4: Systems of Non-Linear Equations

This type of question will test your ability to perform the correct algebraic operations for a given set of equations to find the desired quantity.

PROBLEM

Consider the system of equations
$$x^2 + y^2 = 8$$
$$xy = 4$$
Solve for the quantity $3x + 3y$.

SOLUTION

Solve for the quantity $x + y$ and not for x or y individually.

First, multiply the equation $xy = 4$ by 2 to get $2xy = 8$. Adding this to $x^2 + y^2 = 8$ we obtain

$$x^2 + 2xy + y^2 = 16$$

$$(x + y)^2 = 16$$

$$x + y = 4$$

or $\qquad x + y = -4$

Hence, $3x + 3y = 12$ or $3x + 3y = -12$. We enter 12 for a solution since -12 cannot be entered into the grid.

Question Type 5: Word Problems Involving Hourly Wage

When dealing with this type of question, you will be required to form an algebraic expression from the information based on a person's wages. You will then solve the expression to determine the person's wages (i.e., hourly, daily, annually, etc.).

PROBLEM

Jim works 25 hours a week earning $10 an hour. Sally works 50 hours a week earning y dollars an hour. If their combined income every two weeks is $2,000, find the amount of money Sally makes an hour.

SOLUTION

Be careful. The combined income is given over a two-week period.

Simply set up an equation involving income. We obtain

$$2[(25)(10) + (50)(y)] = 2,000$$

$$[(25)(10) + (50)(y)] = 1,000$$

$$250 + 50y = 1,000$$

$$50y = 750$$

$$y = \$15 \text{ an hour}$$

We enter in the grid

Question Type 6: Word Problems Involving Consecutive Integers

In this type of question, you will need to set up an equation involving consecutive integers based on the product of the integers, which is given.

PROBLEM

Consider two positive consecutive odd integers such that their product is 143. Find their sum.

SOLUTION

Be careful. Notice x and y are consecutive odd integers.

Let

1st odd integer $= x$

2nd odd integer $= x + 2$

We get

$$x(x + 2) = 143$$

$$x^2 + 2x - 143 = 0$$

$$(x - 11)(x + 13) = 0$$

Hence $x = 11$

and $x = -13.$

From the above we obtain the solution sets $\{11, 13\}$ and $\{-13, -11\}$ whose sums are 24 and –24, respectively. Since the problem specifies that the integers are positive, we enter 24.

GEOMETRY AND MEASUREMENT QUESTIONS

In this section, we will explain how to solve questions that test your ability to find the area of various geometric figures. There are six types of questions you may encounter.

Question Type 1: Area of an Inscribed Triangle

This question asks you to find the area of a triangle that is inscribed in a square. By knowing certain properties of both triangles and squares, we can deduce the necessary information.

PROBLEM

Consider the triangle inscribed in the square.

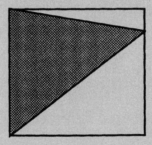

If the area of the square is 36, find the area of the triangle.

SOLUTION

Find the height of the triangle.

Let x be the length of the square. Since the four sides of a square are equal, and the area of a square is the length of a side squared, $x^2 = 36$. Therefore, $x = 6$.

The area of a triangle is given by

$$\tfrac{1}{2} \text{(base) (height).}$$

Here x is both the base and height of the triangle. The area of the triangle is

$$\tfrac{1}{2} (6) (6) = 18.$$

This is how the answer would be gridded.

Question Type 2: Length of the Side of a Triangle

For this type of question, one must find the length of a right triangle given information about the other sides. The key here is to apply the Pythagorean Theorem, which states that the square of the hypotenuse of a right triangle is equal to the sum of the squares of the other two sides.

PROBLEM

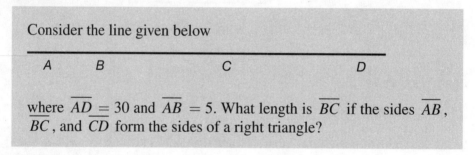

Consider the line given below

where $\overline{AD} = 30$ and $\overline{AB} = 5$. What length is $\overline{BC}$ if the sides $\overline{AB}$, $\overline{BC}$, and $\overline{CD}$ form the sides of a right triangle?

SOLUTION

Draw a diagram and fill in the known information.

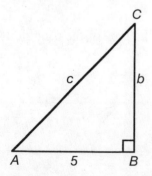

Next, apply the Pythagorean Theorem ($a^2 + b^2 = c^2$), filling in the known variables. Here, we are solving for $\overline{BC}$ (b in our equation). We know that $a = 5$, and since $\overline{AD} = 30$ and $\overline{AB} = 5$, $\overline{BD} = 25$. Filling in these values, we obtain this equation:

$$5^2 + b^2 = (25 - b)^2$$

$$25 + b^2 = 625 - 50b + b^2$$

$$50b = 600$$

$$b = 12$$

This is one possible solution. If we had chosen $c = \overline{CD}$ and $25 - c = \overline{BC}$, one obtains $\overline{BC} = 13$, which is another possible solution. The possible grid entries are shown here.

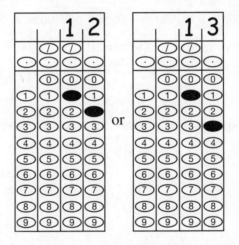

Question Type 3: Solving for the Degree of an Angle

Here you will be given a figure with certain information provided. You will need to deduce the measure of an angle based both on this information, as well as other geometric principles. The easiest way to do this is by setting up an algebraic expression.

PROBLEM

Find the measure of the angle y in the diagram below.

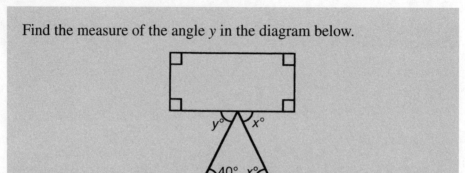

SOLUTION

Use the fact that the sum of the angles on the bottom side of the box is 180°.

Let z be the angle at the top of the triangle. Since we know the sum of the angles of a triangle is 180°,

$$z = 180 - (x + 40).$$

Summing all the angles at the bottom of the square, we get

$$y + [180 - (x + 40)] + x = 180$$

$$y + 140 - x + x = 180$$

$$y + 140 = 180$$

$$y = 40$$

In the grid we enter

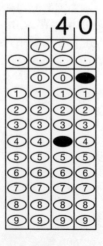

Question Type 4: Solving for the Length of a Side

For this type of question, you will be given a figure with certain measures of sides filled in. You will need to apply geometric principles to find the missing side.

PROBLEM

Consider the figure below.

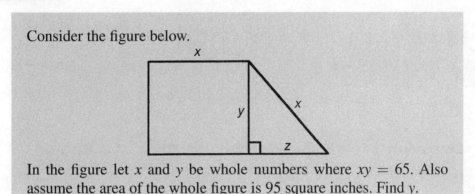

In the figure let x and y be whole numbers where $xy = 65$. Also assume the area of the whole figure is 95 square inches. Find y.

SOLUTION

The key point here is that x and y are whole numbers. Using the figure we only have a finite number of possibilities for z.

The equation for the area of the above figure is

$xy + \frac{1}{2}yz = 95.$

Substituting $xy = 65$ into the above equation, we get

$\frac{1}{2}yz = 30; yz = 60$

Using the fact that $xy = 65$, we know y can be either 1, 5, or 13. As $y = 13$ does not yield a factorization for $yz = 60$, y is either 1 or 5. If $y = 1$, this implies $x = 65$ and $z = 60$ which contradicts the Pythagorean Theorem (i.e., $12 + 602 = 132$). If $y = 5$, this implies $x = 13$ and $z = 12$, which satisfies $y^2 + z^2 = x^2$; hence, the solution is $y = 5$.

In our grid we enter

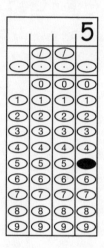

Question Type 5: Solving for the Area of a Region

Here, you will be given a figure with a shaded region. Given certain information, you will need to solve for the area of that region.

PROBLEM

Consider the concentric squares drawn below.

Assume that the side of the larger square is length 1. Also assume that the smaller square's perimeter is equal to the diagonal of the larger square. Find the area of the shaded region.

SOLUTION

The key here is to find the length of the side for the smaller square.

By the Pythagorean Theorem the diameter of the square is

$$d^2 = 1^2 + 1^2$$

which yields $d = \sqrt{2}$. Similarly, the smaller square's perimeter is $\sqrt{2}$; hence, the smaller square's side

$$= \frac{\sqrt{2}}{4}.$$

Calculating the area for the shaded region, we get

$$A = A_{\text{large}} - A_{\text{small}}$$

$$A = 1 - \left(\frac{\sqrt{2}}{4}\right)^2$$

$$A = 1 - \frac{2}{16}$$

$$A = \frac{7}{8}$$

In the grid we enter

Question Type 6: Solving for a Sum of Lengths

The question here involves solving for a sum of lengths in the figure given knowledge pertaining to its area.

PROBLEM

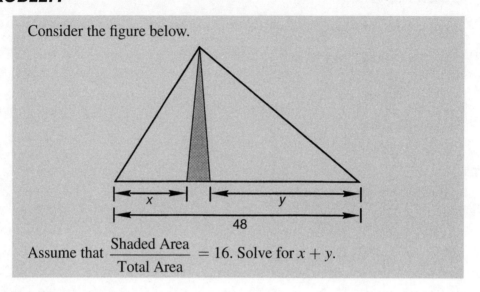

Consider the figure below.

Assume that $\dfrac{\text{Shaded Area}}{\text{Total Area}} = 16$. Solve for $x + y$.

SOLUTION

Solve for $x + y$ and not for x or y individually. Denote by b, the base of the shaded triangle. Then

$$48 - b = x + y.$$

From the information given

$$\frac{\frac{1}{2}48h}{\frac{1}{2}bh} = 16$$

$$\frac{1}{2}48h = 16\left(\frac{1}{2}bh\right)$$

$$24h = 8bh$$

$$24 = 8b$$

$$3 = b$$

Inserting the value for b into our original equation for $x + y$:

$$48 - b = x + y$$

$$48 - 3 = x + y$$

$$45 = x + y$$

We enter in the grid

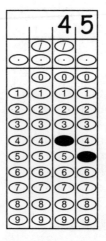

DATA ANALYSIS, STATISTICS, AND PROBABILITY QUESTIONS

This section contains three types of questions you are likely to encounter: data interpretation, statistics, and probability.

Question Type 1: Data Interpretation

As in the Multiple-Choice section, the Student-Produced Response section also will include data interpretation problems. Such problems usually require two basic steps. First, you have to read a chart or graph to obtain certain information. Then you have to apply or manipulate the information to obtain an answer.

PROBLEM

> If there are 88 faculty members between the ages of 30 and 39, what is the combined total of faculty members who are at least 40 years old?

SOLUTION

Because 88 faculty members represents the age bracket 30 to 39, there must be a total of $\frac{88}{0.20}$ = 440 faculty members. The age bracket 40 to 49 represents 100% − 30% − 35% − 20% − 5% = 10% of the total, so that 45% of the faculty is at least 40 years old. (Total of the age brackets 40 to 49, 50 to 59, and over 59.) Thus, (440)(0.45) = 198 faculty members are at least 40 years old. In our grid we enter

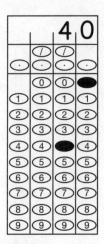

Question Type 2: Statistics

Statistics problems often will ask you to compute the mean, or arithmetic average, of a given set of values. More challenging problems ask you to apply the definition of average. You will recall that the average of a given set of values is equal to the sum of the values divided by the number of values in the set.

PROBLEM

The mean weight for a group of 5 men is 188 pounds. The mean weight for a group of 10 women is 137 pounds. What is the combined mean weight, in pounds, for these two groups?

SOLUTION

The mean weight for all 15 people is total weight divided by $15 = \frac{[(5)(188) + (10)(137)]}{15} = \frac{(940 + 1,370)}{15} = 154$. In our grid we enter

Question Type 3: Probability

Probability problems require you to determine the likelihood that something will occur. As in the sample problem below, the solutions involve simple operations such as percentages, subtractions, and multiplication.

PROBLEM

A jar contains blue, red, and green marbles. There are 36 green marbles and the probability of randomly selecting a green marble is 8%. If the probability of randomly selecting a blue marble is 70%, how many red marbles are in the jar?

SOLUTION

Because 36 green marbles represent 8% of the marbles, there are a total of $\frac{36}{0.08} = 450$ marbles. $100\% - 8\% - 70\% = 22\%$ of the marbles are red, which means there are $(450)(0.22) = 99$ red marbles. In our grid we enter

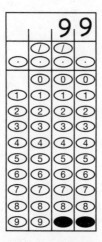

ANSWERING STUDENT-PRODUCED RESPONSE QUESTIONS

When answering Student-Produced Response questions, you should follow these steps.

  Identify the type of question with which you are presented (i.e., arithmetic, algebra, or geometry).

STEP 2   Once you have determined if the question deals with arithmetic, algebra, or geometry, further classify the question. Then, try to determine what type of arithmetic (or algebra or geometry) question is being presented.

STEP 3   Solve the question using the techniques explained in this review. Make sure your answer can be gridded.

STEP 4   Grid your answer in the question's corresponding answer grid. Make sure you are filling in the correct grid. Keep in mind that it is not mandatory to begin gridding your answer on any particular side of the grid. Fill in the ovals as completely as possible, and beware of any stray marks—stray lines may cause your answer to be marked incorrect.

The drill questions that follow should be completed to help reinforce the material that you have just studied. Be sure to refer back to the review if you need help answering the questions.

DRILLS

DIRECTIONS FOR STUDENT-PRODUCED RESPONSE QUESTIONS

For each of the questions below, solve the problem and indicate your answer by marking the ovals in the special grid, as shown in the examples below.

Answer: $\frac{9}{5}$ or 9/5 or 1.8

Either position correct.

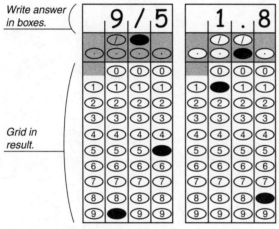

Write answer in boxes.

Grid in result.

Fraction line
Decimal point

- Mark no more than one oval in any column.

- Because the answer sheet will be machine scored, you will receive credit only if the ovals are filled in correctly.

- Although not required, it is suggested that you write your answer in the boxes at the top of the columns to help you fill in the ovals accurately.

- Some problems may have more than one correct answer. In such cases, grid only one answer.

- No question has a negative answer.

- Mixed numbers such as $3\frac{1}{2}$ must be gridded as 3.5 or 7/2.

(If 3|1|/|2 is gridded, it will

be interpreted as $\frac{31}{2}$, not $3\frac{1}{2}$.)

NOTE: You may start your answers in any column, space permitting. Columns not needed should be left

- **Decimal Accuracy:** If you obtain a decimal answer, enter the most accurate value the grid will accommodate. For example, if you obtain an answer such as 0.6666 ..., you should record the result as .666 or .667. Less accurate values such as .66 or .67 are not acceptable.

Acceptable ways to grid $\frac{2}{3}$ = .6666...

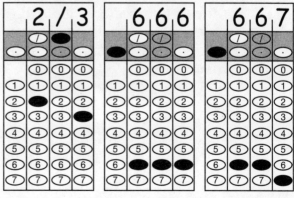

◼ PROBLEM II.1

What does $(-5 - 5) \times (-5 - (-5))$ equal?

SOLUTION

The correct response is:

$$(-5 - 5) \times (-5 - (-5)) = x$$

$$(-5 - 5) \times (-5 + 5) = x$$

$$(-10) \times (0) = x$$

$$0 = x$$

◼ PROBLEM II.2

After 5 tests had been given in a student's biology class, the student had an 82 average (arithmetic mean). After one more test, the student's average was 84. What grade did the student receive on the sixth test?

SOLUTION

The correct response is:

If the student had an average of 82 after 5 tests, then the student accumulated

$82 \times 5 = 410$ points for 5 tests.

After one more test, the student's average was 84. Thus, the student accumulated

$84 \times 6 = 504$ points for 6 tests.

This means that the student would have scored $504 - 410 = 94$ points on the last exam.

■ PROBLEM II.3

At the end of the month, a woman pays $714 in rent. If the rent constitutes 21% of her monthly income, what is her hourly wage given the fact that she works 34 hours per week, and that there are 4 weeks per month?

SOLUTION

The correct response is:

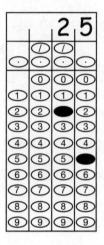

If the rent constitutes 21% of the monthly income, then let x = monthly income and R = rent = \$714.

$R = .21\,x = \$714$

$$x = \frac{714}{.21} = \$3,400$$

Assuming that her monthly income is \$3,400 and that there are 4 weeks in one month, we can calculate her weekly income.

weekly income = \$3,400/month $\times$ month/4 weeks

= \$3,400/4 weeks

= \$850/week

Since the woman works 34 hours per week, her hourly wage can be computed as follows:

\$850/week $\times$ 1week/34 hours = \$850/34 hours

= \$25/hour

◼ PROBLEM II.4

Find the largest integer that is less than 100 and divisible by 3 and 7.

SOLUTION

The correct response is:

Numbers that are divisible by both 3 and 7 are also divisible by 21. We want the largest integer multiple of 21 that is smaller than 100. Multiples of 21 are 21, 42, 63, 84, 105.

84 is the largest multiple that is also less than 100.

■ PROBLEM II.5

The radius of the smaller of two concentric circles is 5 cm, while the radius of the larger circle is 7 cm. Determine the area of the shaded region.

SOLUTION

The correct response is:

The area of the shaded region is equal to the area of the larger circle minus the area of the smaller circle.

area of circle with radius of 7 – area of circle with radius of 5

πr^2 πr^2

$\pi(7)^2$ $\pi(5)^2$

49π 25π

$49\pi - 25\pi = 24\pi$

Since $\pi = 3.14$,

$24\pi = 24(3.14) = 75.36.$

PROBLEM II.6

What is the value of the following?

$$\frac{1}{6} + \frac{2}{3} + \frac{1}{6} - \frac{1}{3} + 1 - \frac{3}{4} - \frac{1}{4} =$$

SOLUTION

The correct response is:

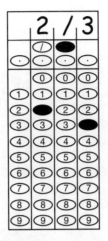

We can simplify this expression by finding a least common denominator (LCD). We see that 12 is the LCD. We then add the numbers from left to right.

$$\frac{1}{6}\times\left(\frac{2}{3}\right)+\frac{2}{3}\times\left(\frac{4}{4}\right)+\frac{1}{6}\times\left(\frac{2}{2}\right)-\frac{1}{3}\left(\frac{4}{4}\right)+1\left(\frac{12}{12}\right)-\frac{3}{4}\left(\frac{3}{4}\right)-\frac{1}{4}\left(\frac{3}{3}\right)=$$

$$=\frac{2}{12}+\frac{8}{12}+\frac{2}{12}-\frac{4}{12}+\frac{12}{12}-\frac{9}{12}-\frac{3}{12}$$

$$=\frac{2+8+2-4+12-9-3}{12}$$

$$=\frac{8}{12}$$

$$=\frac{2}{3}$$

◼ PROBLEM II.7

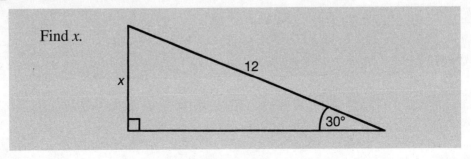

Find x.

12

x

30°

SOLUTION

The correct response is:

This problem can be solved two different ways.

I. $\sin (30°) = (.500) = \dfrac{x}{12}$

We needed to look up the sin of 30°, which is $\dfrac{1}{2}$ or .500.

  $x = (.500)\,(12)$

  $x = 6$

II.   The triangle is a 30° – 60° – 90° triangle. Therefore, the side opposite the 30° angle is equal to half the hypotenuse.

  $x = \dfrac{1}{2}\,\text{hypotenuse}$

  $x = \dfrac{1}{2}\,(12) = 6$

■ PROBLEM II.8

Evaluate the following expression.
$$|-8-4| \div 3 \times 6 + (-4) =$$

SOLUTION

The correct response is:

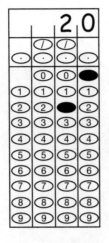

$$|-8 - 4| \div 3 \times 6 + (-4) = |-12| \div 3 \times 6 + (-4)$$
$$= 12 \div 3 \times 6 + (-4)$$
$$= 4 \times 6 + (-4)$$
$$= 24 + (-4) = 20$$

PROBLEM II.9

Let $\overline{RO} = 16$, $\overline{HM} = 30$. Find the perimeter of rhombus *HOMR*.

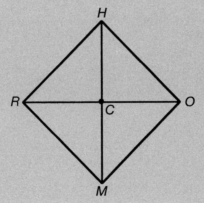

SOLUTION

The correct response is:

Taking the square roots of both sides we have $\overline{RH}$.

$$289 = (\overline{RH})^2$$
$$17 = \overline{RH}$$

Thus, the side of the rhombus has a length $= 17$. Since a rhombus has four equal sides, the perimeter is $4(17) = 68$.

■ PROBLEM II.10

Six years ago, Henry's mother was nine times as old as Henry. Now she is only three times as old as Henry. How old is Henry now?

SOLUTION

The correct response is:

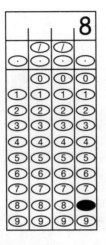

Let x = Henry's age now

   $3x$ = age of Henry's mother now

   $x - 6$ = Henry's age six years ago

   $3x - 6$ = age of Henry's mother six years ago

$$3x - 6 = 9(x - 6)$$
$$3x - 6 = 9x - 54$$
$$3x - 6 + 54 = 9x$$
$$3x + 48 = 9x$$
$$48 = 6x$$
$$\frac{48}{6} = x$$
$$8 = x$$

Henry is now 8 years old.

PROBLEM II.11

If tangerines are sold at the rate of 12 for $1.60 and Sally buys 3 tangerines with a $10.00 bill, and if there is no tax on this transaction, how much change should Sally receive?

SOLUTION

The correct response is:

Let $x =$ the cost of 3 tangerines.

We can set up the following proportion:

$$\frac{12 \text{ tangerines}}{\$1.60} = \frac{3 \text{ tangerines}}{x}$$

$$12x = 3(1.60)$$

$$12x = 4.80$$

$$x = \frac{4.80}{12}$$

$$x = .40$$

Sally pays $0.40 for 3 tangerines.

If she pays with a $10.00 bill, her change is $10.00 − $0.40 = $9.60.

■ PROBLEM II.12

A rectangular desk that measures 32 inches by 77 inches is to be completely covered by pieces of paper. Each piece of paper measures 8 inches by 11 inches. What is the least number of pieces of paper that will be required to cover the desk?

SOLUTION

The correct response is:

Rectangular desk measures 32×77

Piece of paper measures 8×11

It will take exactly 4 pieces of paper to cover the side of the desk that measures 32 inches.

$32 \div 8 = 4$

It will take exactly 7 pieces of paper to cover the side of the desk that measures 77 inches.

$77 \div 11 = 7$

To cover the desk entirely, we need at least $(7)(4) = 28$ pieces of paper.

■ PROBLEM II.13

Five times the smaller of two whole numbers is less than one-fourth the larger number. If the value of the larger number is 84, what is the *largest* possible value of the smaller?

SOLUTION

The correct response is:

Let x = the smaller number

y = the larger number = 84

$$5x < \frac{1}{4}y$$

$$5x < \frac{1}{4}(84)$$

$$5x < 21$$

$$x < \frac{21}{5}$$

$$x < 4\frac{1}{5}$$

Hence, the largest possible integer value of the smaller number is 4.

PROBLEM II.14

The sum of the squares of two consecutive integers is 41. What is the sum of their cubes?

SOLUTION

The correct response is:

Let x = the first integer

$x + 1$ = the next consecutive integer

x^2 = the square of the first integer

$(x + 1)^2 = x^2 + 2x + 1$ = the square of the next consecutive integer

$$(x^2) + (x + 1)^2 = 41$$

$$(x^2) + x^2 + 2x + 1 = 41$$

$$2x^2 + 2x + 1 = 41$$

$$2x^2 + 2x - 40 = 0$$

Dividing both sides of the equation by 2, we get

$$x^2 + x - 20 = 0$$

$$(x - 4)(x + 5) = 0$$

$$x = 4$$

$$x = -5$$

If $x = 4$, then $x + 1 = 5$.

If $x = -5$, then $x + 1 = -4$.

When $x = 4$ and $x + 1 = 5$, the sum of their cubes is

$$4^3 + 5^3 = 64 + 125 = 189.$$

When $x = -5$ and $x + 1 = -4$, the sum of their cubes is

$$(-5)^3 + (-4)^3 = -189.$$

 PROBLEM II.15

A class of 24 students contains 16 males. What is the ratio of females to males?

SOLUTION

The correct response is:

The number of females in the class is equal to the total number of students (24) minus the total number of males (16).

Total number of females $= 24 - 16 = 8$.

The ratio of females to males is

$$\frac{8}{16} = \frac{1}{2}.$$

■ PROBLEM II.16

At an office supply store, customers are given a discount if they pay in cash. If a customer is given a discount of $9.66 on a total order of $276, what is the percentage of the discount?

SOLUTION

The correct response is:

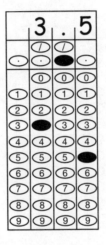

Discount = $9.66

Total order = $276

The percentage of the discount is given by

$$\frac{9.66}{276} = .035$$

To convert .035 to a percentage, we move the decimal over two places to the right and attach the % sign.

Therefore, .035 = 3.5%.

◼ PROBLEM II.17

Solve for x.
$$x + 2y = 8$$
$$3x + 4y = 20$$

SOLUTION

The correct response is:

$$x + 2y = 8 \qquad (1)$$

$$3x + 4y = 20 \qquad (2)$$

We can solve for x in terms of y.

$$x + 2y = 8$$

$$x = 8 - 2y$$

We can substitute this value for x in equation (2).

$$3x + 4y = 20$$

$$3(8 - 2y) + 4y = 20$$

$$24 - 6y + 4y = 20$$

$$-6y + 4y = -4$$

$$-2y = -4$$

$$y = 2$$

Since $y = 2$, we can substitute this value for y in equation (1) to find the value of x.

$$x + 2y = 8 \qquad (2)$$

$$x + 2(2) = 8$$

$$x + 4 = 8$$

$$x = 4$$

■ PROBLEM II.18

Find a prime number less than 40 that is of the form $5k + 1$.

SOLUTION

The correct response is:

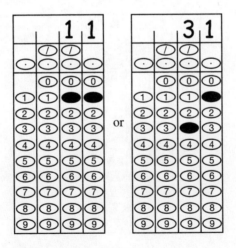

To find a prime number less than 40 that is of the form $5k + 1$, we consider the positive integers that are of the form $5k + 1$ and are less than 40.

For $k = 0$ $\qquad 5k + 1 = 5(0) + 1 = 1$

$k = 1$ $\qquad 5(1) + 1 = 6$

$k = 2$ $\qquad 5(2) + 1 = 11$ (prime)

$$k = 3 \qquad 5\,(3) + 1 = 16$$

$$k = 4 \qquad 5\,(4) + 1 = 21$$

$$k = 5 \qquad 5\,(5) + 1 = 26$$

$$k = 6 \qquad 5\,(6) + 1 = 31 \text{ (prime)}$$

$$k = 7 \qquad 5\,(7) + 1 = 36$$

The prime numbers in this set are 11 and 31.

■ PROBLEM II.19

Find the value of the expression.

$$\frac{7}{10} \times \frac{4}{21} \times \frac{25}{36} =$$

SOLUTION

The correct response is:

$$\frac{7}{10} \times \frac{4}{21} \times \frac{25}{36} = \frac{1}{10} \times \frac{4}{3} \times \frac{25}{36}$$

$$= \frac{1}{10} \times \frac{1}{3} \times \frac{25}{9}$$

$$= \frac{1}{2} \times \frac{1}{3} \times \frac{5}{9}$$

$$= \frac{1}{6} \times \frac{5}{9}$$

$$= \frac{5}{54}$$

■ PROBLEM II.20

Find the solution for x in the pair of equations.

$$x + y = 7$$

$$x = y - 3$$

SOLUTION

The correct response is:

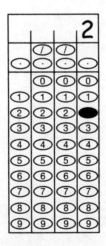

$$x + y = 7 \qquad (1)$$

$$x = y - 3 \qquad (2)$$

We can substitute the value for x in equation (2) into equation (1).

$$x + y = 7 \qquad (1)$$

$$(y - 3) + y = 7$$

$$2y - 3 = 7$$

$$2y = 10$$

$$y = 5$$

Substituting $y = 5$ into equation (2), we get

$$x = y - 3 \qquad (2)$$

$$x = 5 - 3$$

$$x = 2$$

■ PROBLEM II.21

Simplify.

$$\frac{\frac{1}{2} + \frac{1}{3}}{\frac{1}{6}}$$

SOLUTION

The correct response is:

$$\frac{\frac{1}{2} + \frac{1}{3}}{\frac{1}{6}}$$

We must first simplify the numerator.

$$\frac{1}{2}\left(\frac{3}{3}\right) + \frac{1}{3}\left(\frac{2}{2}\right) = \frac{3}{6} + \frac{2}{6} = \frac{5}{6}$$

We now have

$$\frac{\frac{5}{6}}{\frac{1}{6}}$$

$$\frac{5}{6} \div \frac{1}{6} = \frac{5}{6} \times \frac{6}{1} = 5$$

■ PROBLEM II.22

For the triangle pictured below, the degree measures of the three angles are x, $3x$, and $3x + 5$. Find x.

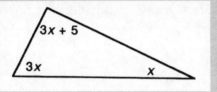

SOLUTION

The correct response is:

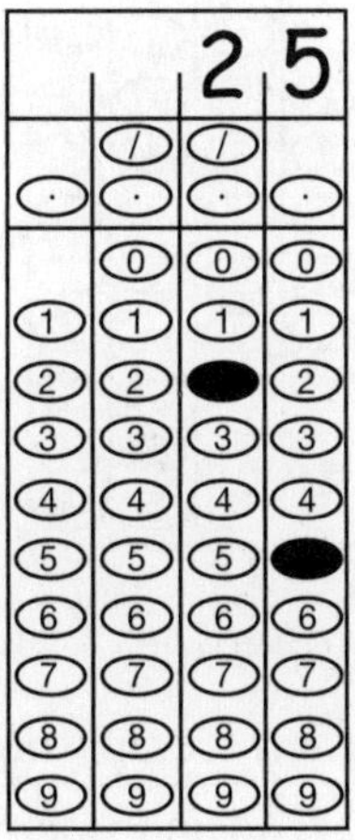

The sum of the angles of a triangle must add up to $180°$.

$$x + 3x + (3x + 5) = 180°$$
$$7x + 5 = 180°$$
$$7x = 175°$$
$$x = \frac{175°}{7} = 25°$$

■ PROBLEM II.23

In an apartment building there are 9 apartments having terraces for every 16 apartments. If the apartment building has a total of 144 apartments, how many apartments have terraces?

SOLUTION

The correct response is:

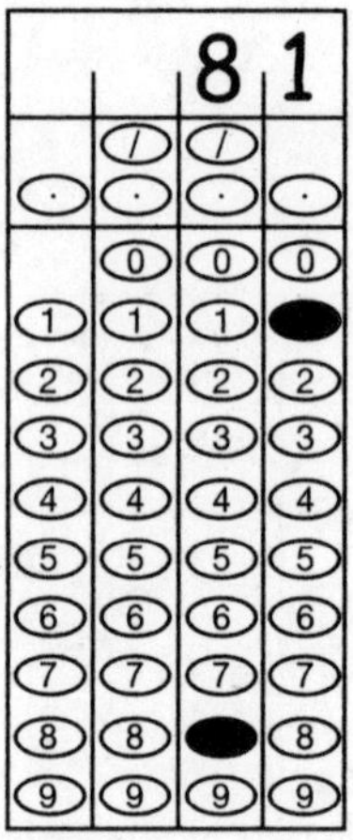

We can set up the following proportion:

$$\frac{9 \text{ terrace apartments}}{16 \text{ apartments}} = \frac{x \text{ terrace apartments}}{144 \text{ apartments}}$$

Cross multiplying, we have:

$$9(144) = 16x$$
$$1,296 = 16x$$
$$\frac{1,296}{16} = x$$
$$81 = x$$

PROBLEM II.24

Solve the equation
$$2x^2 - 5x + 3 = 0.$$

SOLUTION

The correct response is:

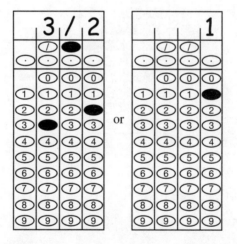

$$2x^2 - 5x + 3 = 0$$

We factor the left side of the equation, set each of these factors to zero, and solve for x.

$$(2x - 3)(x - 1) = 0$$

$$2x - 3 = 0 \qquad x - 1 = 0$$

$$2x = 3 \qquad\qquad x = 1$$

$$x = \frac{3}{2}$$

The solutions are $\frac{3}{2}$ and 1.

PROBLEM II.25

Solve the proportion
$$\frac{x+1}{4} = \frac{15}{12}.$$

SOLUTION

The correct response is:

$$\frac{x+1}{4} = \frac{15}{12}$$

To solve the proportion, we cross multiply.

$$(x + 1)12 = 4(15)$$

$$12x + 12 = 60$$

$$12x = 48$$

$$x = 4$$

PROBLEM II.26

What is the smallest even integer n for which $(.5)^n$ is less than $.01$?

SOLUTION

The correct response is:

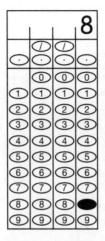

To find the smallest even integer n for which $(.5)^n$ is less than $.01$, we start by looking at the positive even powers of $.5$.

When $n = 0$ $\quad (.5)^0 = 1$

$\qquad n = 2$ $\quad (.5)^2 = .25$

$\qquad n = 4$ $\quad (.5)^4 = .0625$ $\qquad$ These values are all $> .01$

$\qquad n = 6$ $\quad (.5)^6 = .015625$

$\qquad n = 8$ $\quad (.5)^8 = .00390625$

The answer therefore is $n = 8$.

■ PROBLEM II.27

In the correctly worked multiplication problem below, M, N, and P are nonzero digits.

$$\begin{array}{r} M \\ \times 8 \\ \hline NP \end{array}$$

If the value of N is 3, then what is the value of M?

SOLUTION

The correct response is:

We are given that M, N, and P are nonzero numbers and

$$\begin{array}{r} M \\ \times 8 \\ \hline NP \end{array}$$

When $N = 3$

$$\begin{array}{r} M \\ \times 8 \\ \hline 3P \end{array}$$

Thus, M must be a number that gives thirty-something when multiplied by 8. Trial and error is the best method here.

Try $M = 3$. This gives $3 \times 8 = 24$.

Try $M = 4$. This gives $4 \times 8 = 32$.

Try $M = 5$. This gives $5 \times 8 = 40$.

Thus, the only possible answer is $M = 4$.

▪ PROBLEM II.28

A chef bought a jar that holds 76.25 gallons of liquid. How many quart containers are required to fill the jar? (1 gallon = 4 quarts)

SOLUTION

The correct response is:

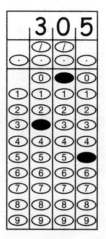

There are 4 quarts in a gallon. To find the number of quarts in the jar, we must multiply the number of quarts in a gallon (4) by the number of gallons in the jar (76.25).

$$4 \times (76.25) = 305 \text{ quart containers}$$

◼ PROBLEM II.29

The following shows the bank account balance of Mr. Jones on various dates.

December 1	+ $75.50
December 8	− $53.36
December 15	+ $62.28

What, to the nearest dollar, is the arithmetic mean of the account balances?

SOLUTION

The correct response is:

To find the arithmetic mean, we must add the bank account balances and then divide by the number of dates.

$$\text{mean} = \frac{(\$75.50) + (-\$53.36) + (\$62.28)}{3}$$

$$\text{mean} = \frac{\$84.42}{3}$$

$$\text{mean} = \$28.14$$

To the nearest dollar, $28.14 rounds off to $28.

◼ PROBLEM II.30

If
$$m^{15} = \frac{48}{y} \text{ and } m^{13} = \frac{2}{6y} \text{ and } m > 0,$$
what is the value of m?

SOLUTION

The correct response is:

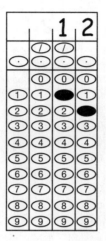

$$m^{15} = \frac{48}{y}$$

$$m^{13} = \frac{2}{6y}$$

m^{15} and m^{13} are powers of the same base.

$$\frac{m^{15}}{m^{13}} = m^2 = \frac{\frac{48}{y}}{\frac{2}{6y}} = \frac{48}{y} \div \frac{2}{6y} = \frac{48}{y} \times \frac{6y}{2}$$

$$m^2 = 144$$

$$m = \sqrt{144} = 12$$

■ PROBLEM II.31

When 8 consecutive integers are multiplied, their product is 0. What is their maximum sum?

SOLUTION

The correct response is:

If the product of 8 integers is zero, we know that at least one of the integers must be zero.

Since the integers are *consecutive*, no more than one of the integers can equal zero.

Here are a few examples of sets of integers that meet the above requirements:

$$-7, -6, -5, -4, -3, -2, -1, 0$$

and $-3, -2, -1, 0, 1, 2, 3, 4$

and $0, 1, 2, 3, 4, 5, 6, 7$

The problem asks for the maximum sum.

The more negative numbers we include, the smaller our sum will be.

Thus, the maximum sum equals

$$0 + 1 + 2 + 3 + 4 + 5 + 6 + 7 + 8 = 28$$

◼ PROBLEM II.32

Four numbers are selected at random. They have an average (arithmetic mean) of 47. The third number selected was 12. What is the sum of the other three numbers?

SOLUTION

The correct response is:

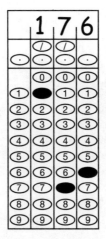

If four numbers have an average of 47, their sum would be the product of the average multiplied by the number of numbers.

$$47 \times 4 = 188$$

If the third number equals 12, then the sum of the remaining three numbers must equal the total sum minus 12.

$$188 - 12 = 176$$

The sum of the other three numbers equals 176.

■ PROBLEM II.33

$$\frac{y}{27} = \frac{3}{y}$$

What is the largest possible value of y that would solve the equation above?

SOLUTION

The correct response is:

To solve this problem for y, we must cross multiply.

$$y^2 = 3(27)$$

$$y^2 = 81$$

$$y = \sqrt{81} = \pm 9$$

We find that y can equal $+9$ or -9. The larger value is $y = 9$.

◼ PROBLEM II.34

Square A has a side of $\sqrt{6}$ and square B has a side of 6. How much greater is the area of square B than the area of square A?

SOLUTION

The correct response is:

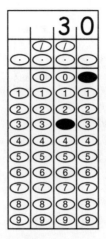

To find out how much greater the area of square B is than the area of square A, we must first find the area of each square, and then subtract the area of square A from the area of square B.

Area of a square $= (\text{side})^2$

Area of square $A = (\sqrt{6}\,)^2 = 6$

Area of square $B = (6)^2 = 36$

Area of Square B – Area of Square $A = 36 - 6 = 30$

■ PROBLEM II.35

The product of 7 and n is 11 more than m. If $n = 6$, what is the value of m?

SOLUTION

The correct response is:

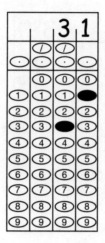

We know that the product of 7 and n is 11 more than m. We can set up the following equation:

$7 \times n = m + 11$

We can now substitute $n = 6$ into the equation.

$7 \times (6) = m + 11$

We can now simplify the equation and solve for m.

$42 = m + 11$

$42 - 11 = m + 11 - 11$

$31 = m$

▮ PROBLEM II.36

What would 20% of $3x$ be, if 60% of x were 15?

SOLUTION

The correct response is:

If 60% of x is 15, we get

$$60\% \times x = 15$$

$$.60x = 15$$

$$x = \frac{15}{.60}$$

$$x = 25$$

$3x$ is then $3\,(25) = 75$.

20% of $3x$ = 20% of 75

$$= .20 \times 75$$

$$= 15$$

■ PROBLEM II.37

A gym teacher enters the swimming pool area at 8:30 A.M. and notices that the water in the pool is only 1.5 feet deep. State regulations require that the water be at least 5 feet deep. If the water flowing into the pool raises the water level at a rate of .25 feet per hour, how many hours will it take to fill the pool to the height required by state law?

SOLUTION

The correct response is:

If the water is 1.5 feet deep and it must be 5 feet deep, the gym teacher must add $5 - 1.5 = 3.5$ feet of water.

If the water raises the level .25 feet per hour and we want to find out how long it would take to raise the water level by 3.5 feet, we must divide the amount we need the water raised (3.5 feet) by the amount the water will be raised each hour (.25 feet).

$$3.5 \div .25 = 14$$

It will take 14 hrs.

■ PROBLEM II.38

If $a = 10$, $b = 50$, and $c = a \times b$, what is the decimal value of $\frac{1}{c}$?

SOLUTION

The correct response is:

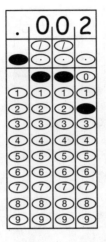

$$a = 10$$

$$b = 50$$

$$c = a \times b$$

$$c = 10 \times 50$$

$$c = 500$$

Therefore,

$$\frac{1}{c} = \frac{1}{500}$$

To express $\frac{1}{500}$ as a decimal, we divide the numerator by the denominator:

$$1.000 \div 500 = .002$$

Therefore, $\frac{1}{c} = .002$

■ PROBLEM II.39

What is the number of minutes in a day, rounded to the nearest hundred?

SOLUTION

The correct response is:

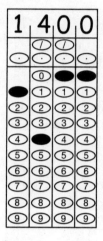

One day has 24 hours.

One hour has 60 minutes.

To find out how many minutes are in a day, we multiply the number of hours in a day by 60.

24 hours/day $\times$ 60 min/hour = 1,440 min/day

Rounded to the nearest hundred, we have 1,400 minutes.

◼ PROBLEM II.40

In a school, 18 students take math and 12 take biology. If there are a total of 22 students enrolled in the school, how many students take both math and biology?

SOLUTION

The correct response is:

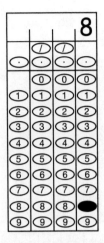

Let x = number of students who take math and biology

y = number taking math alone

z = number taking biology alone

$$x + y = 18$$

$$x + z = 12$$

$$x + y + z = 22$$

We can substitute $(x + y) = 18$ into the last equation.

$$18 + z = 22$$

$$z = 4$$

Four equals the number of students taking biology alone.

If $z = 4$ and $x + z = 12$, we can solve for x.

$$x + z = 12$$

$$x + 4 = 12$$

$$x = 8$$

This is the number of students who are taking both math and biology.

■ PROBLEM II.41

The mean (average) of the numbers 50, 60, 65, 75, x, and y is 65.
What is the mean of x and y?

SOLUTION

The correct response is:

If the average of the 6 numbers is 65, we have the following equation:

$$\frac{50 + 60 + 65 + 75 + x + y}{6} = 65$$

$$250 + x + y = (65)6$$

$$x + y = 390 - 250$$

$$x + y = 140$$

If the sum of x and y is 140, then the mean of x and y is

$$\frac{140}{2} = 70 .$$

PROBLEM II.42

The ages of the students enrolled at XYZ University are given in the following table:

Age	Number of students
18	750
19	1,600
20	1,200
21	450

What percentage of students are 19 and 20 years old?

SOLUTION

The correct response is:

$$\frac{\text{number of 19-year-olds} + \text{number of 20-year-olds}}{\text{total number of students}} =$$

$$= \frac{1,600 + 1,200}{750 + 1,600 + 1,200 + 450} = \frac{2,800}{4,000}$$

$$= \frac{7}{10} = .70$$

To find the percentage, we move the decimal point two places to the right and add the % sign.

$$\frac{7}{10} = .70 = 70\%$$

◼ PROBLEM II.43

Find the larger side of a rectangle whose area is 24 and whose perimeter is 22.

SOLUTION

The correct response is:

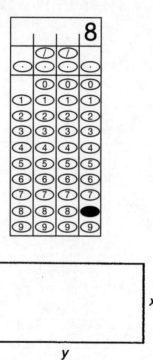

Let x = smaller side of the rectangle (length)

Let y = larger side of the rectangle (width)

Area = (length)(width)

$24 = xy$

Perimeter = 2(length) + 2(width)

$22 = 2x + 2y$

We can simplify this equation by dividing both sides by 2.

$11 = x + y$

We can now solve for y in terms of x. We see that

$y = (11 - x)$

Substituting this value for y in the area equation, we get

$24 = x(11 - x)$

$24 = 11x - x^2$

We can now set one side equal to zero.

$x^2 - 11x - 24 = 0$

We can now factor and set each of the factors equal to zero.

$(x - 8)(x - 3) = 0$

$x - 8 = 0 \qquad x - 3 = 0$

$x = 8 \qquad x = 3$

If $x = 8$, then $y = 3$

since $xy = 24$

$8y = 24$

$y = 3$

Likewise:

If $x = 3$, then $y = 8$.

The value of the larger side is therefore 8.

■ PROBLEM II.44

The following are three students' scores on Mr. Page's Music Fundamentals midterm. The given score is the number of correct answers out of 55 total questions.

Liz	48
Jay	45
Carl	25

What is the *average* percentage of questions correct for the three students?

SOLUTION

The correct response is:

To find the average number of correct questions, we must add the scores obtained by each student and then divide by the number of students.

$$\frac{48 + 45 + 25}{3} = \frac{118}{3} = 39\frac{1}{3}$$

$39\frac{1}{3}$ is the average number of correct questions.

To find the average percentage of correct questions, we divide the average number of correct questions by the total number of questions.

$$\frac{39\frac{1}{3}}{55} = \frac{\frac{118}{3}}{55} = \frac{118}{165} = .715 = 71.5\%$$

▪ PROBLEM II.45

Reserved seat tickets to a football game are $6 more than general admission tickets. Mr. Jones finds that he can buy general admission tickets for his whole family of five for only $3 more than the cost of reserved seat tickets for himself and Mrs. Jones. How much do the general admission tickets cost?

SOLUTION

The correct response is:

Let x = price of a general admission seat

$x + 6$ = price of a reserved seat

Therefore $5x$ = price of general admission seats for five people

$2(x + 6)$ = cost of reserved seats for Mr. and Mrs. Jones

Thus, we can say

$5x = 2(x + 6) + 3$

$5x = 2x + 12 + 3$

$5x = 2x + 15$

$3x = 15$

$x = 5$

$5.00 is the price for general admission seats.

◼ PROBLEM II.46

The sum of three numbers is 96. The ratio of the first to the second is 1:2, and the ratio of the second to the third is 2:3. What is the third number?

SOLUTION

The correct response is:

Let x = first number

y = second number

z = third number

$$x + y + z = 96$$

$$\frac{x}{y} = \frac{1}{2}$$

$$\frac{y}{z} = \frac{2}{3}$$

Solving for y in the third equation, we see that

$$y = \frac{2z}{3}.$$

Likewise, solving for x in the second equation, we get

$$x = \frac{y}{2} = \frac{\frac{2z}{3}}{2} = \frac{z}{3}.$$

Plugging both of these terms into the first equation, we obtain

$$\frac{z}{3} + \frac{2z}{3} + z = 96$$

$$2z = 96$$

$$z = 48$$

■ PROBLEM II.47

If $L_1 \parallel L_2$ and L_4 and L_1 are tangents to the circle, then what does angle f equal?

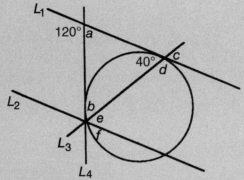

Note: Figure not drawn to scale.

SOLUTION

The correct response is:

The sum of the angles of a line is 180°. Because angle a and the 120° angle form L_1, they must add up to 180°.

$$a + 120° = 180°$$

$$a = 60°$$

If $L_1 \parallel L_2$, then angle a is equal to angle f. This is because corresponding angles of parallel lines are equal.

Therefore, $f = 60°$

■ PROBLEM II.48

Last Valentine's Day 100 red roses cost r dollars. This Valentine's Day, 80 of the same kind of red rose cost $.2r$ dollars. If there were no discounts based on the size of the purchase, what was the percentage decrease in the cost of a red rose?

SOLUTION

The correct response is:

80 red roses cost $.2r$ dollars.

$$80 = .2r$$

$$\frac{80}{.2} = r$$

$$400 = r$$

This means that this year r dollars will buy 400 roses. To find the percentage change, we must first compute how much 100 red roses would cost at this year's price.

$$\frac{r}{400} = \frac{x}{100}$$

$$100r = 400x$$

$$\frac{100r}{400} = x$$

$$\frac{r}{4} = x$$

$$.25r = \frac{r}{4} = x$$

Since 100 roses cost r dollars last year, but 100 roses cost $.25r$ this year, the percentage decrease in value of a rose would be the difference in value between the cost of 100 roses last year and 100 roses this year.

$$1.00r - .25r = .75r$$

This value represents a decrease of 75%.

■ PROBLEM II.49

In the figure shown below, if the average (arithmetic mean) of $\overline{FG}$ and $\overline{GH}$ is 12.2, what is the distance from point G to point H?

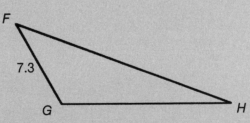

Note: Figure not drawn to scale.

SOLUTION

The correct response is:

$$\text{Average} = \frac{\overline{FG} + \overline{GH}}{2} = 12.2$$

$$\overline{FG} + \overline{GH} = 24.4$$

Since $\overline{FG} = 7.3$

$$7.3 + \overline{GH} = 24.4$$

Therefore, solving for $\overline{GH}$, we get

$$\overline{GH} = 24.4 - 7.3 = 17.1.$$

PROBLEM II.50

The list price of a new car was $10,000. During a sale, the car was sold for $7,500. By what percentage was the original price of the car reduced?

SOLUTION

The correct response is:

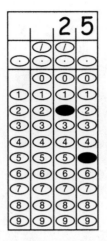

Let $x =$ percentage of decrease

$$\frac{\text{amount of decrease}}{\text{original amount}} = x\%$$

$$\frac{10,000 - 7,500}{10,000} = \frac{x}{100}$$

$$\frac{2,500}{10,000} = \frac{x}{100}$$

$$100x = 2,500$$

$$x = 25$$

■ PROBLEM II.51

Two consecutive even integers have a sum of 26. What is the result when they are multiplied?

SOLUTION

The correct response is:

Let x = first even integer

$x + 2$ = second even integer

$x + (x + 2) = 26$

$2x + 2 = 26$

$2x = 24$

$x = 12$

$x + 2 = 14$

$(x)(x + 2) = (12)(14) = 168$

■ PROBLEM II.52

On Sunday there are 15 restaurants open in the city. Each restaurant serves an average (arithmetic mean) of 1,200 customers. On the following day, 7 of the restaurants close for a holiday, but the same number of people use the restaurants. What is the increase in the average number of customers at each restaurant?

SOLUTION

The correct response is:

If the 15 restaurants served an average of 1,200 customers, then the 15 restaurants served a total of

15 × 1,200 or 18,000 customers.

If 7 of 15 restaurants close, then 8 would remain open.

If 18,000 customers were served by 8 restaurants, then each served an average of

$\dfrac{18,000}{8}$ or 2,250 customers.

If on Sunday each restaurant averaged 1,200 customers and on Monday each restaurant averaged 2,250 customers, the increase in the average number of customers at each restaurant is

2,250 − 1,200 = 1,050 customers.

■ PROBLEM II.53

An ancient map indicates that treasure is buried 300 feet below the bottom of a mountain 1,500 feet high, the peak of which is 2,750 feet above the bottom of a cliff located close to the mountain. If the map is accurate, how many feet above the bottom of the cliff is the treasure located?

SOLUTION

The correct response is:

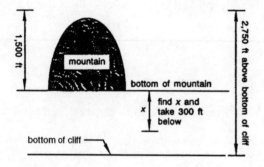

The peak of the mountain is 2,750 ft above the bottom of the cliff.

The mountain is 1,500 ft high. Therefore, the height of the bottom of the mountain relative to the bottom of the cliff is

$$2,750 - 1,500 = 1,250.$$

The treasure was buried 300 feet below the bottom of the mountain.

$$1,250 - 300 = 950$$

This is the location of the treasure relative to the bottom of the cliff.

■ PROBLEM II.54

Define ¥ by the following equations:
$m \text{¥} n = 2m + n$, where $n > 0$.
$m \text{¥} n = m - 2n$, where $n \leq 0$.
What is the value of the following expression:
$6 \text{¥} - 4$?

SOLUTION

The correct response is:

$m \text{¥} n = 2m + n$, where $n > 0$

$m \text{¥} n = m - 2n$, where $n \leq 0$

We must consider that the symbol ¥ changes according to the value of n. In the expression $6 \text{¥} -4$, the number to the right of ¥ is -4. This is less than zero. We must therefore use the second equation.

The second equation says that we are to take the number to the left of ¥ (in this case 6) and from that number subtract twice the number to the right of ¥ (in this case -4).

$m - 2n$

$6 - 2(-4)$

$$6 - (-8)$$

$$6 + 8 = 14$$

■ PROBLEM II.55

If m is an integer and the sum of m and the next integer larger than m is greater than 10, what is the smallest possible value of m?

SOLUTION

The correct response is:

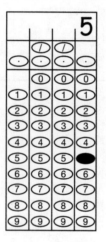

Let m = an integer

$m + 1$ = the next larger integer

$$m + (m + 1) > 10$$

$$2m + 1 > 10$$

$$2m > 10 - 1$$

$$2m > 9$$

$$m > \frac{9}{2}$$

$$m > 4.5$$

The smallest integer greater than 4.5 is 5.

▪ PROBLEM II.56

If the sum of the digits of a two-digit positive whole number is 8 and the tens digit is three times the units digit, then what is the two-digit number?

SOLUTION

The correct response is:

Let u = the units digit

t = the tens digit

$u + t = 8$

$t = 3u$

Substituting $t = 3u$ for t in $u + t = 8$, we get

$u + t = 8$

$u + 3u = 8$

$4u = 8$

$u = 2$

The units digit is 2.

Substituting this value for u into either of the equations above, we get

$$u + t = 8 \qquad t = 3u$$
$$2 + t = 8 \qquad t = 3 \times 2$$
$$t = 6 \qquad t = 6$$

The tens digit is 6.

The number therefore is 62.

◼ PROBLEM II.57

In the diagram below, $L1 \parallel L2$ and $L3 \parallel L4$. If $a + d + b = 8e$, what is the measure of angle e?

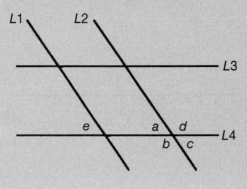

SOLUTION

The correct response is:

$$\angle c = \angle a$$

vertical angles are equal.

$$\angle e = \angle a$$

corresponding angles of parallel lines are equal.

$$\angle c = \angle e$$

since angles equal to the same angle are equal to each other.

$$\angle a + \angle b + \angle c + \angle d = 360$$

since $\qquad \angle c + \angle d = 180$

and $\qquad \angle a + \angle b = 180.$

We are given that

$$\angle a + \angle d + \angle b = 8(\angle e).$$

Then substituting we get

$$8(\angle e) + \angle c = 360°$$
$$8(\angle e) + \angle e = 360°$$
$$9(\angle e) = 360°$$
$$\angle e = \frac{360°}{9} = 40°$$

■ PROBLEM II.58

Find the length of a side of an equilateral triangle whose area is $4\sqrt{3}$.

SOLUTION

The correct response is:

The area of an equilateral triangle is

$$\frac{1}{2}bh.$$

Using the Pythagorean Theorem we have

$$b^2 = \left(\frac{b}{2}\right)^2 + h^2$$

$$b^2 = \frac{b^2}{4} + h^2$$

$$\frac{3b^2}{4} = h^2$$

$$\frac{\sqrt{3}b}{2} = h$$

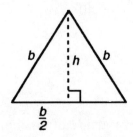

Substituting

$$h = \frac{\sqrt{3}b}{2}$$

into $\quad \frac{1}{2}bh = 4\sqrt{3}$

$$\frac{1}{2}\frac{\sqrt{3}b^2}{2} = 4\sqrt{3}$$

$$b^2 = 16$$

$$b = 4$$

◼ PROBLEM II.59

Solve

$$\frac{3}{x-1} + \frac{1}{x-2} = \frac{5}{(x-1)(x-2)}.$$

SOLUTION

The correct response is:

$$\frac{3}{x-1} + \frac{1}{x-2} = \frac{5}{(x-1)(x-2)}$$

$$(x-1)(x-2)\frac{3}{x-1} + (x-1)(x-2)\frac{1}{x-2} = \frac{5}{(x-1)(x-2)}(x-1)(x-2)$$

This simplifies to

$$3(x-2) + (x-1) = 5$$

$$3x - 6 + x - 1 = 5$$

$$4x - 7 = 5$$

$$4x = 12$$

$$x = 3$$

■ PROBLEM II.60

In an isosceles triangle, the length of each of the congruent sides is 10 and the length of the base is 12. Find the length of the altitude drawn to the base.

SOLUTION

The correct response is:

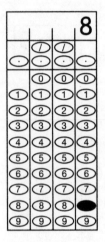

In order to find the altitude A, we use the Pythagorean Theorem.

The altitude divides the base in half.

$6^2 + A^2 = 10^2$

$36 + A^2 = 100$

$A^2 = 64$

$A = 8$

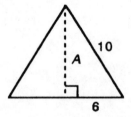

■ PROBLEM II.61

$\triangle PQR$ is a scalene triangle. The measure of $\angle P$ is eight more than twice the measure of $\angle R$. The measure of $\angle Q$ is two less than three times the measure of $\angle R$. Determine the measure of $\angle Q$.

SOLUTION

The correct response is:

In a scalene triangle the three sides are not equal.

Let x = measure of $\angle R$

$2x + 8$ = measure of $\angle P$

$3x - 2$ = measure of $\angle Q$

Since the sum of the angles in a triangle = 180°, then

$$\angle P + \angle Q + \angle R = 180°$$

$$(2x + 8) + (3x - 2) + x = 180°$$

$$6x + 6 = 180$$

$$6x = 174$$

$$x = 29$$

Therefore,

$$\angle Q = 3x - 2$$

$$= 3\,(29) - 2$$

$$= 87 - 2$$

$$= 85°$$

■ PROBLEM II.62

A mother is now 24 years older than her daughter. In 4 years, the mother will be 3 times as old as the daughter. What is the present age of the daughter?

SOLUTION

The correct response is:

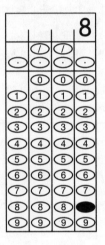

Let x = daughter's age now

$x + 4$ = daughter's age in 4 years

$x + 24$ = mother's age now

$(x + 24) + 4$ = mother's age in 4 years

$(x + 24) + 4 = 3 (x + 4)$

$x + 28 = 3x + 12$

$28 = 2x + 12$

$16 = 2x$

$8 = x$

The present age of the daughter is 8.

■ PROBLEM II.63

John is four times as old as Harry. In six years John will be twice as old as Harry. What is Harry's age now?

SOLUTION

The correct response is:

Let x = Harry's age now

$4x$ = John's age now

$x + 6$ = Harry's age in 6 years

$4x + 6$ = John's age in 6 years

$4x + 6 = 2(x + 6)$

$4x + 6 = 2x + 12$

$2x = 6$

$x = 3$

Harry is now 3 years old.

■ PROBLEM II.64

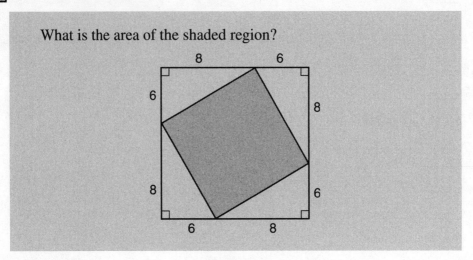

What is the area of the shaded region?

SOLUTION

The correct response is:

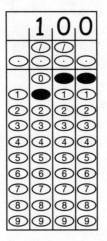

The area of the shaded region is the total area of the square minus the area of the four right triangles.

The area of the square = (side)^2.

The side of the square is $(8 + 6) = 14$.

The area of the square is $14^2 = 196$.

The areas of the triangles can be determined using the equation

$\dfrac{1}{2}bh.$

The area of the triangles is

$\dfrac{1}{2}(8)(6) = 24.$

Since there are four triangles, the total area of the triangles is

$4(24) = 96.$

The area of the shaded region is therefore

$196 - 96 = 100.$

■ PROBLEM II.65

In the diagram shown, ABC is an isosceles triangle. Sides $\overline{AB}$ and $\overline{BC}$ are extended through C to E and D to form triangle CDE. What is the sum of the measures of angles D and E?

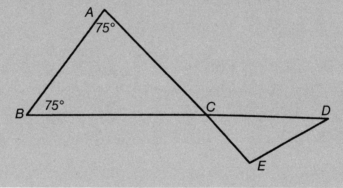

SOLUTION

The correct response is:

The sum of the angles in a triangle is $180°$.

$$\angle CAB + \angle ABC + \angle BCA = 180°$$

$$75° + 75° + \angle BCA = 180°$$

$$150° + \angle BCA = 180$$

$$\angle BCA = 30°$$

Since $\angle ACB$ is a vertical angle to $\angle DCE$, then $\angle ACB = \angle DCE = 30$.

In triangle CDE we have

$$\angle D + \angle E + \angle DCE = 180°$$

$$\angle D + \angle E + 30° = 180°$$

$$\angle D + \angle E = 150°$$

◼ PROBLEM II.66

Number of Muffins	Total Price
1	$0.55
Box of 4	$2.10
Box of 8	$4.00

According to the information in the table above, what would be the *least* amount of money needed to purchase exactly 19 muffins? (Disregard the dollar sign when gridding your answer.)

SOLUTION

The correct response is:

In order to make good use of the discount we want to first buy boxes of eight, then boxes of four, and then buy single muffins. This minimizes the price.

Two boxes of eight muffins gives us a total of

$2 \times 8 = 16$ muffins, plus $3 \times$ single muffins

would give us the 19 muffins.

$$2(\$4.00) + 3\,(\$0.55) = \$8.00 + \$1.65$$

$$= \$9.65$$

■ PROBLEM II.67

> Several people rented a van for $30, sharing the cost equally. If there had been one more person in the group, it would have cost each $1 less. How many people were there in the group originally?

SOLUTION

The correct response is:

Let x = number of people renting the van

y = cost to each person

$xy = 30$

By adding one more person to the van, the cost per person goes down by $1.

This means that

$x + 1$ = new number of people renting the van for $30

$y - 1$ = new cost per person

Now

$(x + 1)(y - 1) = 30.$

Substituting $xy = 30$ into this equation gives

$$(x+1)(y-1) = xy$$
$$xy - x + y - 1 = xy$$
$$-x + y - 1 = 0$$
$$y = x + 1$$

Since $xy = 30$, we can substitute $y = x + 1$ into this equation.

$$x(x + 1) = 30$$
$$x^2 + x = 30$$
$$x^2 + x - 30 = 0$$
$$(x + 6)(x - 5) = 0$$

$$x + 6 = 0 \qquad\qquad x - 5 = 0$$
$$x = -6 \qquad\qquad x = 5$$

Since the number of people in the van cannot be a negative number, the answer is 5.

■ PROBLEM II.68

Find the area of the shaded triangles.

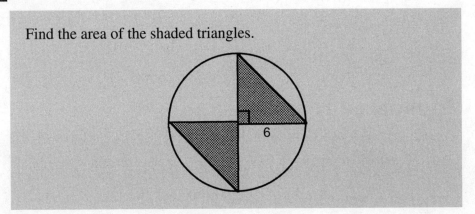

SOLUTION

The correct response is:

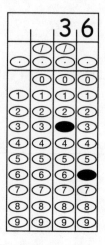

We are given that the radius of the circle is 6. The area of the shaded region is the area of the two triangles.

The area $= \dfrac{1}{2} bh.$

The base and height of the triangle equal the radius.

$$\frac{1}{2} bh = \frac{1}{2}(6)(6) = 18$$

The area of two triangles is

$$2 \times 18 = 36.$$

■ PROBLEM II.69

Given the rhombus *RHOM*, find the length of the diagonal $\overline{RO}$.

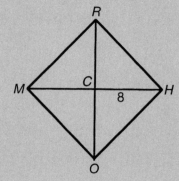

SOLUTION

The correct response is:

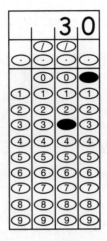

The diagonals of a rhombus meet at right angles.

Since $\overline{CH} = 8$ and $\overline{RH} = 17$, we can solve for $\overline{RC}$ using the Pythagorean Theorem as follows:

$$(\overline{CH})^2 + (\overline{RC})^2 = (\overline{RH})^2$$

$$8^2 + (\overline{RC})^2 = 17^2$$

$$64 + (\overline{RC})^2 = 289$$

$$(\overline{RC})^2 = 289 - 64$$

$$(\overline{RC})^2 = 225$$

$$\overline{RC} = 15$$

Therefore,

$$\overline{RO} = \overline{RC} + \overline{CO}$$

$$\overline{RO} = 15 + 15 = 30$$

■ PROBLEM II.70

$\triangle MNO$ is isosceles. If the vertex angle, $\angle N$, has a measure of 96°, find the measure of $\angle M$.

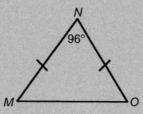

Note: Figure not drawn to scale.

SOLUTION

The correct response is:

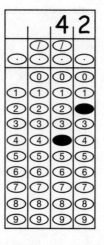

In an isosceles triangle two sides are equal.

$$\overline{MN} = \overline{NO} \text{ and } \angle M = \angle O$$

Since the sum of the angles of a triangle equals 180, we have

$$\angle N + \angle M + \angle O = 180°$$
$$96° + 2(\angle M) = 180°$$
$$2(\angle M) = 180° - 96°$$
$$2(\angle M) = 84°$$
$$\angle M = 42°$$

■ PROBLEM II.71

The sum of two integers is 31, and the difference between the two integers is 7. What is the larger of the two integers?

SOLUTION

The correct response is:

Let x = first integer

y = second integer

$x + y = 31$ (1)

$x - y = 7$ (2)

We can solve equation (1) for x.

$x + y = 31$

$x = 31 - y$

We can now substitute this value for x in equation (2).

$x - y = 7$

$(31 - y) - y = 7$

$31 - 2y = 7$

$$24 = 2y$$

$$12 = y$$

We can now substitute this value into either equation (1) or equation (2) to give us the value of x.

$$x + y = 31$$

$$x + 12 = 31$$

$$x = 31 - 12 = 19$$

Since $12 < 19$, the larger of the two integers is 19.

■ PROBLEM II.72

In the figure below, if $\angle e = 135$, what is the value of $\angle f + \angle g$?

SOLUTION

The correct response is:

$\angle e = 135°$

$\angle e = \angle i$

because vertical angles are equal.

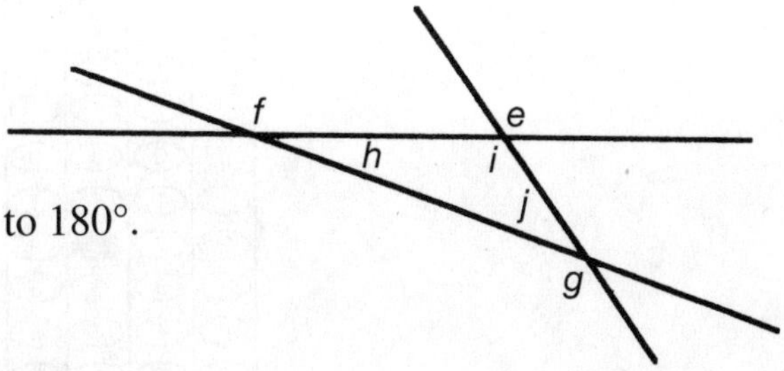

$\angle h + \angle f = 180$

$\angle j + \angle g = 180$

Supplementary angles add up to 180°.

$\angle h = 180 - \angle f$

$\angle j = 180 - \angle g$

$\angle i + \angle j + \angle h = 180$

The sum of the angles of a triangle is 180°.

Substituting:

$$135 + (180 - \angle g) + (180 - \angle f) = 180°$$

$$495 - \angle g - \angle f = 180°$$

$$495 - 180 - \angle g - \angle f = 0$$

$$315 = \angle g + \angle f$$

◼ PROBLEM II.73

If $\frac{1}{4}$ of an even positive number and $\frac{5}{6}$ of the next larger even number have a sum of 32, what is the average of the two numbers?

SOLUTION

The correct response is:

Let $x =$ first even positive number

$x + 2 =$ second even positive number

$$\frac{1}{4}x + \frac{5}{6}(x+2) = 32$$

We must now solve for x.

$$\frac{1}{4}x + \frac{5x+10}{6} = 32$$

$$\frac{3}{3}\left(\frac{1}{4}x\right) + \frac{2}{2}\left(\frac{5x+10}{6}\right) = 32$$

$$\frac{3x}{12} + \frac{10x+20}{12} = 32$$

$$\frac{3x+10x+20}{12} = 32$$

$$13x + 20 = (32)12$$

$$13x + 20 = 384$$

$$13x = 384 - 20$$

$$13x = 364$$

$$x = \frac{364}{13}$$

$$x = 28$$

The numbers are 28 and 30.

The average of the two numbers is

$$\frac{28 + 30}{2} = 29.$$

◼ PROBLEM II.74

A crop duster reading a map learns that on the map she must treat a circular area of 9π sq. in. If 30 miles on the ground is represented by 1 inch on the map, the area in square miles that the crop duster must treat is _____ π?

SOLUTION

The correct response is:

The area on the map that the crop duster must treat is 9π sq. in. We can compute the radius of the circle as follows:

Area of circle $= \pi r^2$

$9\pi = \pi r^2$

$9 = r^2$

$3 = r$

The radius on the map is 3 inches. Since 1 inch is equal to 30 miles, we can set up a proportion to determine the radius of the circle on the ground.

$$\frac{30}{1} = \frac{x}{3}$$

$$x = 3\,(30)$$

$$x = 90$$

Thus, the radius of the circle on the ground is 90. Using this information we can now compute the area of the circle on the ground.

$$\text{Area of circle} = \pi r^2$$

$$\text{Area} = \pi(90)^2$$

$$\text{Area} = 8{,}100\pi \text{ sq. miles}$$

■ PROBLEM II.75

A soccer team has played 22 games of which it has won 13 and lost 9. If the team wins its remaining z games and finishes the season with a 70% winning percentage, what is the value of z?

SOLUTION

The correct response is:

The number of games won divided by the total number of games played is equal to the winning percentage.

$$\frac{\text{number of games won}}{\text{total number of games played}} = \text{winning percentage}$$

$$\frac{13+z}{22+z} = 70\%$$

$$\frac{13+z}{22+z} = .70$$

$$\frac{13+z}{22+z} = \frac{70}{100}$$

$$100(13+z) = 70(22+z)$$

$$1,300 + 100z = 1,540 + 70z$$

$$30z = 240$$

$$z = \frac{240}{30}$$

$$z = 8$$

The team must win the next 8 games.

■ PROBLEM II.76

What would be the value of y if $\sqrt{81} = 3^y$?

SOLUTION

The correct response is:

$$\sqrt{81} = 3^y \qquad \sqrt{81} = 9$$

$$9 = 3^y$$

We must write 9 with a base of 3 to solve for y.

$$3^2 = 3^y$$

$$2 = y$$

■ PROBLEM II.77

A student received a grade of A on 6 out of every 36 tests she took during her junior year. In fractional form, what was the ratio of non-A to A grades that the student received during her junior year?

SOLUTION

The correct response is:

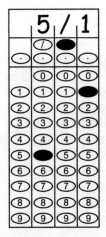

We know that the student received a grade of A on 6 tests out of a total of 36 tests. The student received a non-A grade on $36 - 6$ tests $= 30$ tests.

Therefore the ratio

$$\frac{\text{non-A grades}}{\text{A grades}} = \frac{30}{6} = \frac{5}{1}$$

■ PROBLEM II.78

Eleven minutes is what fractional part of 11 hours?

SOLUTION

The correct response is:

11 hours × 60 min/hr = (11) (60) min

$$= 660 \text{ min}$$

Hence, eleven minutes is

$$\frac{11}{660} \text{ of 11 hours.}$$

So eleven minutes is $\frac{1}{60}$ of 11 hours.

■ PROBLEM II.79

The PTA of a certain school has 150 members. The PTA wishes to form a number of committees on which exactly 10 people will serve. If no one may serve on more than two committees, what is the maximum number of committees that may be formed?

SOLUTION

The correct response is:

If the PTA has 150 members who will be divided up into committees of 10 people, then the number of committees that could be formed would be

$$\frac{150}{10} = 15 \text{ committees}$$

Since no one person may serve on more than two committees, then each of the 15 committees could create two committees. There would then be $15 \times 2 = 30$ possible committees.

■ PROBLEM II.80

To induce camaraderie, a teacher has decided that each member of his English class will shake the hand of every other student of the English class at the beginning of each class. If there are 12 students in attendance, how many handshakes will there be?

SOLUTION

The correct response is:

One way to visualize the problem is that one person shakes everyone's hand and then leaves the room. Then a second person shakes the hand of everyone in the room, and then that person leaves the room. We continue to do this until there is one person left in the room.

The first person will shake 11 hands. The second person will shake 10 hands. With 10 students in the room, the third student will shake 9 hands. We can see that a pattern is developing. Each time we increase the number of students doing the handshaking by one, we also decrease the number of handshakes by one.

# handshakes	11	10	9	8	7	6	5	4	3	2	1	0
person number	1	2	3	4	5	6	7	8	9	10	11	12

The number of handshakes is

$$11 + 10 + 9 + 8 + 7 + 6 + 5 + 4 + 3 + 2 + 1 = 66.$$

For 12 students there will be 66 handshakes.

■ PROBLEM II.81

The letters below represent consecutive integers on a number line.

$$a \quad b \quad c \quad d \quad e \quad f \quad g \quad h \quad i \quad j$$

If $2b + f = 13$, what is the value of b.

SOLUTION

The correct response is:

On a number line the numbers become greater as we move to the right.

Since the letters represent consecutive integers and f is four spaces to the right of b, we can say that $b + 4 = f$

$$2b + f = 13$$

$$2b + (b + 4) = 13$$

$$2b + b + 4 = 13$$

$$3b + 4 = 13$$

$$3b = 9$$

$$b = 3$$

■ PROBLEM II.82

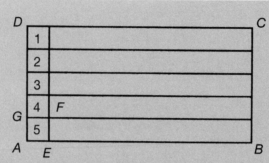

If *ABCD* is a rectangle and squares 1 through 5 each have an area of 4, $\overline{EB}$ and $\overline{AE} = 6$, what is the area of *ABCD*?

SOLUTION

The correct response is:

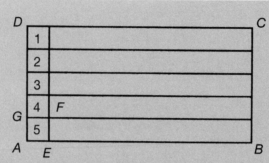

Since *AEFG* is a square with an area of 4, then each of its sides must equal 2. This is because the area of a square $= s^2$. Thus, $\overline{AG} = 2$.

Because $\overline{AG}$ is 2 and $\overline{AD}$ is 5 times as long as $\overline{AG}$,

$$\overline{AD} = 5 \times 2 = 10.$$

We also know that $\overline{EB} = 6\ \overline{AE}$. We know that $\overline{AE} = 2$, because all sides of a square are equal.

$$\overline{EB} = 6\ \overline{AE}$$

$$\overline{EB} = 6 \times z$$

$$\overline{EB} = 12$$

Also,

$$\overline{AE} + \overline{EB} = \overline{AB}$$

$$2 + 12 = \overline{AB}$$

$$14 = \overline{AB}$$

Thus, $\overline{AB} = 14$ and $\overline{AD} = 10$.

$$\text{Area} = \text{length} \times \text{width}$$

$$\text{Area } ABCD = \overline{AB} \times \overline{AD}$$

$$= 14 \times 10$$

$$= 140$$

■ PROBLEM II.83

If $6y + 3x + 8xy - 94 = 0$ and $x + 5 = 13$, then $y + 4 = ?$

SOLUTION

The correct response is:

$$6y + 3x + 8xy - 94 = 0$$

$$x + 5 = 13$$

We can solve for x.

$$x + 5 = 13$$

$$x = 13 - 5$$

$$x = 8$$

We can now substitute this value for x in the first equation.

$$6y + 3x + 8xy - 94 = 0$$

$$6y + 3(8) + 8(8)y - 94 = 0$$

$$6y + 24 + 64y - 94 = 0$$

$$70y - 70 = 0$$

$$70y = 70$$

$$y = \frac{70}{70}$$

$$y = 1$$

Therefore, $y + 4 = 1 + 4 = 5$.

■ PROBLEM II.84

Two people are 33 miles apart. They begin to walk towards each other along a straight line at the same time. If one walks at the rate of 4 miles per hour while the other walks at the rate of 7 miles per hour, in how many hours will they meet?

SOLUTION

The correct response is:

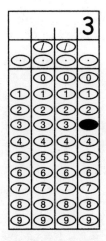

Since this problem involves distance between two points, we use the distance formula.

Distance = rate × time

We know that the distance of the first walker plus the distance of the second walker is 33 miles.

Distance of 1st walker + Distance of 2nd walker = 33

We are given that the rate of the first walker is 4 miles/hr and that of the second walker is 7 miles/hr.

(rate) (time of 1st walker) + (rate) (time of 2nd walker) = 33

4 (time of 1st walker) + 7(time of 2nd walker) = 33

We know that both walkers walked for the same length of time, which we will label T.

Thus,

$$4T + 7T = 33$$

$$11T = 33$$

$$T = 3 \text{ hours}$$

They each walked for 3 hours.

■ PROBLEM II.85

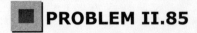

What is the largest integer for which $(a + 3)(a - 7)$ is negative?

SOLUTION

The correct response is:

$(a + 3)(a - 7)$ is negative

For the product of $(a + 3)(a - 7)$ to be negative, one of the terms must be positive and the other must be negative.

In looking at the terms $(a + 3)$ and $(a - 7)$, we can see that $(a + 3)$ will always be greater than $(a - 7)$.

Because $(a + 3)$ is a greater term, we want to find out the range of the values for which $(a + 3)$ will be positive. That is, $(a + 3) > 0$.

$a + 3 > 0$

$a + 3 - 3 > 0 - 3$

$a > -3$

Thus, if $a > -3$, then $(a - 3)$ will be positive.

Now we must determine when $(a - 7)$ will be negative,

$a - 7 < 0$

$a - 7 + 7 < 0 + 7$

$a < 7$

Thus, the product of $(a - 7)$ and $(a + 3)$ will be negative when $a < 7$ and $a > -3$.

$-3 < a < 7$

Therefore, the largest integer that will yield a negative number for $(a - 7)$ and a positive number for $(a + 3)$ would be 6.

PROBLEM II.86

A student reaching into a refrigerator realizes that the solid container on the top shelf has a volume of $\frac{4}{5}\pi^2 x^8$. Before closing the refrigerator, the student also notices that the solid container on the bottom shelf of the refrigerator has a volume of $\frac{5}{4}\pi^2 x^8$. What percent of the container on the bottom shelf is the container on the top shelf?

SOLUTION

The correct response is:

$$\frac{\text{container on top shelf}}{\text{container on bottom shelf}} = \frac{\frac{4}{5}\pi^2 x^8}{\frac{5}{4}\pi^2 x^8}$$

$$= \frac{\frac{4}{5}}{\frac{5}{4}}$$

$$= \frac{4}{5} \times \frac{4}{5} = \frac{16}{25}$$

$$= .64$$

$$= 64\%$$

■ PROBLEM II.87

A coach informed his team that the average score for players on the team was m. The coach further said that the average score for the first 15 players was 70. There were 25 players on the team, and the range of the scores was from 60 to 100, inclusive. What is the greatest possible difference between the highest and lowest possible values of m?

SOLUTION

The correct response is:

The first 15 players had an average score of 70. These 15 players scored exactly $70 \times 15 = 1,050$ points.

Since there were 25 players in total on the team, there were $25 - 15 = 10$ remaining players. To find the lowest possible value of m, which is the lowest possible average, we must assume that each of the 10 remaining players produced the lowest possible score.

The lowest possible score was 60. If each of the remaining 10 players scored 60, these 10 players would have scored $(60)(10) = 600$ points.

The total low score for all 25 players is $1,050 + 600 = 1,650$ points.

1,650 points scored by 25 people would be an average of $1,650 \div 25$ or 66 points per player.

To find the highest possible value of m, which is the highest possible average, we must assume that the 10 remaining players produced the highest score possible.

The highest possible score was 100. If each of the remaining 10 players scored 100, these 10 players would have scored $10 \times 100 = 1,000$ points.

The total high score for all 25 players would be $1,050 + 1,000$ or 2,050 points.

2,050 points scored by 25 players would average $2,050 \div 25$ or 82 points per team member.

Thus, the highest possible average would be 82 and the lowest would be 66. Thus, the difference is $82 - 66 = 16$ points.

■ PROBLEM II.88

A child has six tiles. Each tile is emblazoned with one of the following letters: *G, H, I, J, K,* or *L*. How many different three-letter arrangements (such as *HKG*) can the child create if *G* is always the last letter in the arrangement and one of the letters in the arrangement is *K*?

SOLUTION

The correct response is:

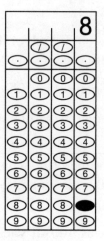

We note that the order of the letters is important in the problem since *G* must always be last and *K* must be one of the other two letters.

We can first write all the arrangements where *K* is the first letter and *G* is the last letter.

{*KHG, KIG, KJG, KLG*} 4 arrangements

Then we write all the arrangements where *K* is the second letter and another letter, other than *K* or *G,* is the first letter.

{*HKG, IKG, JKG, LKG*} 4 arrangements

This gives a total of 8 arrangements where *G* is always the last letter and one of the letters in the arrangement is *K*.

■ PROBLEM II.89

What is the smallest positive integer that is divisible by each of the following numbers: 3, 4, 5, and 6?

SOLUTION

The correct response is:

We are being asked to find the least common multiple. To do this take the highest number, 6, and then ask whether 3, 4, and 5 goes evenly into multiples of 6. The lowest number for which this occurs will be the answer.

We see that 60 is divisible by 5, 4, and 3.

Therefore, 60 is the smallest positive integer that is divisible by 3, 4, 5, and 6.

■ PROBLEM II.90

If, in the equations below, $h = 6$, then what is the value of g?

$$2g + 4h + 6i = 22$$
$$2h + 2i = 10$$

SOLUTION

The correct response is:

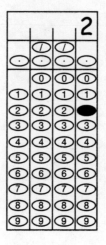

$$2g + 4h + 6i = 22 \quad (1)$$

$$2h + 2i = 10 \quad (2)$$

$$h = 6$$

Substitute $h = 6$ in equation (2)

$$2(6) + 2i = 10$$

$$12 + 2i = 10$$

$$2i = -2$$

$$i = -1$$

We know now that $h = 6$ and $i = -1$. We can substitute these values into equation (1).

$$2g + 4h + 6i = 22$$

$$2g + 4(6) + 6(-1) = 22$$

$$2g + 24 - 6 = 22$$

$$2g + 18 = 22$$

$$2g = 4$$

$$g = 2$$

■ PROBLEM II.91

If $m + 2m + 3m = 20 + m$, then what does $m = ?$

SOLUTION

The correct response is:

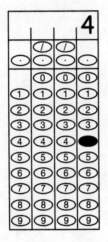

$$m + 2m + 3m = 20 + m$$

Combining like terms, we get

$$6m = 20 + m$$

$$6m - m = 20$$

$$5m = 20$$

$$m = \frac{20}{5}$$

$$m = 4$$

■ PROBLEM II.92

$$
\begin{array}{r}
35M \\
+NM \\
\hline
M28
\end{array}
$$

In the above correctly added addition problem, each letter stands for exactly one number. What is the value of N?

SOLUTION

The correct response is:

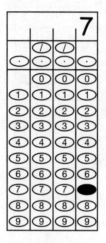

Reading down the column on the far right, we see

$M + M =$ a number that ends in 8.

What values of M are possible?

If $M = 4$, $M + M = 8$ (a number that ends in 8).

If $M = 9$, $M + M = 18$ (a number that ends in 8).

Thus, $M = 4$ or 9 are the two possible values.

First let's try $M = 4$ to see if the given addition problem will work out correctly when we use this value. We substitute 4 for M every place where M appears. This gives

$$
\begin{array}{r}
354 \\
+N4 \\
\hline
428
\end{array}
$$

What values of N are possible when $M = 4$?

Reading down the middle column, we see

$5 + N =$ a number that ends in 2.

(We did *not* need to carry any value over from the column on the far right, since our choice $M = 4$ implies $M + M = 8$. In the case where $M = 9$, and $M + M = 18$, we would need to carry a 1.)

Trying different values for N in the expression $5 + N$, we find $N = 7$ is the only value for N that results in a number ending in 2. The next step is to substitute 7 for N, to see if the addition works for these values.

$$\begin{array}{r} 354 \\ +74 \\ \hline 428 \end{array}$$

The addition is correct, so $M = 4$ and $N = 7$ are correct. If you were to go back to the beginning and repeat the same process using $M = 9$, you would not get a correct sum.

The answer to this problem is thus $N = 7$.

■ PROBLEM II.93

A child draws three triangles in the sand and labels them triangle A, triangle B, and triangle C. Triangle A is three times the area of triangle B, triangle B is three times the area of triangle C, and triangle B has an area of 3. If the areas of all three triangles are added together, what would be their sum?

SOLUTION

The correct response is:

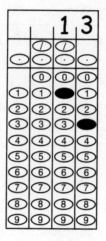

area $\Delta B = 3$

area $\Delta A = 3(\text{area } \Delta B) = 3 \times 3 = 9$

area $\Delta B = 3(\text{area } \Delta C)$

If B is 3 times C, to make C and B equal, we must divide B by 3.

Therefore,

$$\text{area } \Delta C = \frac{\text{area } \Delta B}{3} = \frac{3}{3}$$

area $\Delta C = 1$

Thus, the sum of the area equals

$$1 + 3 + 9 = 13.$$

■ PROBLEM II.94

For all numbers c and d, let $\lozenge$ be defined by the following equation
$$c \lozenge d = d^2 + cd - c.$$
If $3 \lozenge g = 25$, what is the positive value of g?

SOLUTION

The correct response is:

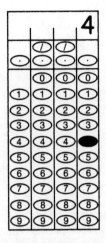

If $\lozenge$ defines the relationship of the values on either side, then

$$c \lozenge d = d^2 + cd - c$$

and $\ 3 \lozenge g = g^2 + 3g - 3$

(meaning $c = 3$, $d = g$ by the definition)

$$= g^2 + 3g - 3$$

According to the statement of the problem

$$3 \lozenge g = g^2 + 3g - 3 = 25$$

(Solving this equation for g, set the right side equal to zero by adding -25 to both sides.)

$$g^2 + 3g - 28 = 0$$

(Factor the left side)

$$(g + 7)(g - 4) = 0$$

(Set each factor equal to zero)

$$g + 7 = 0 \qquad g - 4 = 0$$

$$g = -7 \qquad g = 4$$

Since the question asks for the positive value of g, $g = 4$.

■ PROBLEM II.95

A list of numbers has been arranged such that each number in the list is 8 less than the number that precedes it. If 105 is the ninth number in the list, what is the fourth number in the list?

SOLUTION

The correct response is:

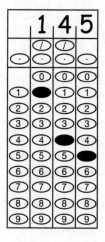

We need to set up a list of 9 numbers. The ninth number is 105. Each number on the list is 8 less than the number that precedes it. We can fill in the list as follows:

1st	2nd	3rd	4th	5th	6th	7th	8th	9th
159	141	153	145	137	129	121	113	105

The fourth number on the list is 145.

■ PROBLEM II.96

Two identical humidifers vaporize water at exactly the same uniform rate. Each humidifier has been filled to its maximum capacity. It takes exactly 8 hours for each humidifier to completely vaporize a tank of water. The first humidifier is turned on at exactly 6:00 P.M. The second humidifier is turned on exactly one hour later. How many hours will it take before the water remaining in the second tank is twice the water remaining in the first tank?

SOLUTION

The correct response is:

We can consider the following chart. Since we are told that the tanks require 8 hours to completely vaporize water, and because they vaporize at a uniform rate, we may assume that each tank holds 8 gallons of water, and therefore, each humidifier vaporizes 1 gal of water each hour.

Before humidifier is turned on	First Tank–8 gal	Second Tank–8 gal
End of 1 hr	7 gal	8 gal
End of 2 hrs	6 gal	7 gal
End of 3 hrs	5 gal	6 gal
End of 4 hrs	4 gal	5 gal
End of 5 hrs	3 gal	4 gal
End of 6 hrs	2 gal	3 gal
End of 7 hrs	1 gal	2 gal

After 7 hours there are twice as many gallons in the second tank as in the first tank.

 **PROBLEM II.97**

> The price of a compact disc player was reduced from $200.00 to $147.59. What was the percentage decrease in the price of the unit?

SOLUTION

The correct response is:

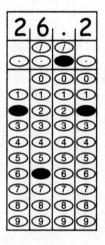

The price of the compact disc player was reduced from $200 to $147.59. The amount of decrease is

$$\$200.00 - \$147.59 = \$52.41$$

The percentage decrease is the

amount of the decrease
───────────────────
original amount of unit

$$\frac{52.41}{200.00} = .26205$$

To obtain a percent from a fraction we move the decimal point two places to the right.

$$.26205 = 26.205\%$$

◼ PROBLEM II.98

In triangle ABC, $\overline{AB} = 6$ and $\overline{AC} = 9.2$. If $\overline{BC}$ is an integer, what is the smallest possible perimeter of the triangle?

SOLUTION

The correct response is:

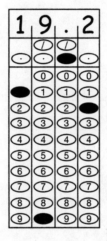

To find the smallest possible perimeter, we must find the smallest possible value for side $\overline{BC}$.

When any two sides of a triangle are added together, the sum of these two sides must be greater than the third side.

Thus,

$$\overline{BC} + \overline{AB} > \overline{AC}$$

$$\overline{BC} + 6 > 9.2$$

$$\overline{BC} > 9.2 - 6$$

$$\overline{BC} > 3.2$$

We are told that $\overline{BC}$ is an integer. The smallest integer greater than 3.2 is 4. Thus, the smallest possible value of $\overline{BC}$ is 4.

The perimeter of the triangle is therefore

$$\overline{AB} + \overline{AC} + \overline{BC} = 6 + 9.2 + 4$$

$$= 19.2$$

◼ PROBLEM II.99

A bus driving at an average speed of 55 miles per hour takes the basketball team to a game in 4 hours. Because of snowy weather conditions, while following the same route home, the bus must average 40 miles per hour. How many minutes more will the return trip take than the original trip?

SOLUTION

The correct response is:

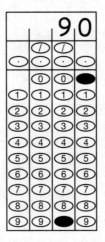

Since the bus averages 55 miles per hour for 4 hours, the length of the trip is found using the distance formula.

Distance = rate × time

$$= 55 \times 4 = 220 \text{ miles}$$

Because the bus followed the same route, the return trip must also be 220 miles. We can now substitute into the distance formula to compute the time.

$$D = R \times T$$

$$220 = 40 \times T$$

$$220 = 40T$$

$$\frac{220}{40} = T$$

$$5.5 = T$$

Therefore, the return trip took 5.5 hours. The return trip was 1.5 hrs longer. $(5.5 - 4.0 = 1.5)$

Finally, we can convert 1.5 hours into minutes by multiplying by the number of minutes in an hour.

$$60 \times 1.5 = 90$$

■ PROBLEM II.100

If a teacher travels from point M to point O, by first passing through point N, the teacher will have traveled a distance of 225 miles. If the rate of travel while going from point M to point N is 15 miles per hour and the rate of travel while going from point N to point O is 30 miles per hour, and the trip has a total travel time of 9 hours, what is the distance, in miles, from point N to point O?

SOLUTION

The correct response is:

The distance from point M to point O plus the distance from point N to point O equals 225.

Distance MN + Distance $NO = 225$

rate $\times$ time (of MN) + rate $\times$ time (NO) = 225

$15 \times$ time (of MN) + $30 \times$ time (NO) = 225

We are given that it took 9 hours for the trip.

Let time of $MN = x$

time of $NO = 9 - x$

Substituting these values in the above equation, we get

$$15 \times x + 30 \times (9 - x) = 225$$

$$15x + 270 - 30x = 225$$

$$270 - 225 - 15x = 0$$

$$45 = 15x$$

$$3 = x$$

$$6 = 9 - x$$

Hence, the time to cover distance $MN = 3$ hours and the time to cover distance $NO = 6$ hrs.

Distance $NO = (30 \text{ miles/hr}) \ 6 \text{ hr}$

$$= 180 \text{ miles}$$

■ PROBLEM II.101

Ken and Joanne are painting a boat. If each person were working alone, Joanne would need twice as much time to paint this boat as Ken would need. Together, they can finish this paint job in 8 hours. After 3 hours of working together, what fraction of the entire paint job has Ken completed?

SOLUTION

The correct response is:

Let x = time alone needed by Ken and let $2x$ = time alone needed by Joanne. Then $\frac{8}{x} + \frac{8}{2x} = 1$. Multiply the equation by $2x$ to get $16 + 8 = 2x$. Then, $x = 12$. Ken would need 12 hours if he were working alone. After 3 hours, he has completed $\frac{3}{12} = \frac{1}{4}$ of the work.

■ PROBLEM II.102

The length of a shed is 8 feet more than its width. If the perimeter of the shed is 36 feet, what is the area of the shed in square feet?

SOLUTION

The correct response is:

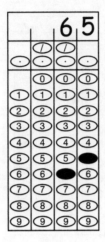

Denote the length by a and the width by b. Then, $2(a + b) = 36$ and $a = b + 8$. Solving these equations, we get $a = 13$ and $b = 5$. These measures give the area of the shed: $5 \times 13 = 65$ square feet.

■ PROBLEM II.103

The height of a free-falling object is given by the equation $H = x - 16t^2$, where H is the height in feet at any time, t is the time in seconds, and x is the initial height in feet. An object is dropped from a height of 1,000 feet. After approximately how many seconds will it attain a height of 200 feet?

SOLUTION

The correct response is:

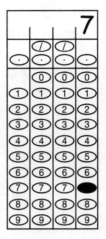

By substitution, $200 = 1000 - 16t^2$, $-800 = -16t^2$, and $t^2 = 50$. So, $t = \sqrt{50} \approx 7$.

■ PROBLEM II.104

A survey was taken in three different regions of Iowa. In it, people were asked to name the most important issue that needs to be addressed by politicians. The results are shown below.

	Crime	Taxes	Schools
Region 1	45%	20%	35%
Region 2	30%	55%	15%
Region 3	50%	40%	10%

The number of people surveyed in Regions 1, 2, and 3 were 200, 300, and 500, respectively. What is the total number of people who chose the issue of crime from Region 1, schools from Region 2, and taxes from Region 3?

SOLUTION

The correct response is:

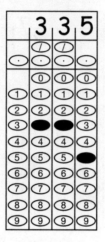

We calculate $(.45)(200) + (.15)(300) + (.40)(500) = 335$.

■ PROBLEM II.105

A wheel with a radius of $\frac{50}{\pi}$ inches is rolled along the ground. It makes 3 revolutions per second. How many <u>feet</u> does it travel in 26 seconds?

SOLUTION

The correct response is:

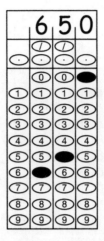

One revolution = circumference = $(2\pi)\left(\frac{50}{\pi}\right)$ = 100 inches. 3 revolutions per second = 300 inches per second. Then, in 26 seconds, the wheel travels $(300)(26) = 7800$ inches. Finally, 7800 inches = $\frac{7800}{12}$ = 650 feet.

PROBLEM II.106

In the figure below, if $RS = PR$ and $PQ = 6$, what is the length of SQ? (Round your answer to the nearest tenth).

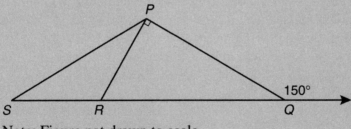

Note: Figure not drawn to scale.

SOLUTION

The correct response is:

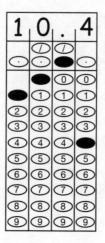

$\angle PQR = 180° - 150° = 30°$, so $\triangle PQR$ is a $30° - 60° - 90°$ right triangle. Let x = length of PR, so $2x$ = length of QR. Recall that in a $30° - 60° - 90°$ right triangle, the side opposite the $30°$ angle is one-half the hypotenuse. Then $x^2 + 6^2 = (2x)^2$, $x^2 + 36 = 4x^2$ $3x^2 = 36$, $x^2 = 12$, $x = 2.128 = PR$. So $QR = 2(2.128)$, and since $PR = RS$, $RS = 12$. Now $SQ = QR + RS = 3(2.128) \approx 10.4$.

■ PROBLEM II.107

The population growth of a type of bacteria that begins with a count of A and grows by a factor of 6 every t years is given by the formula $B = (A)(6^{y/t})$, where y represents the number of years of growth and B represents the growth after y years. Suppose the population was 800 in the year 1900. By the year 1990, the population was 172,800. What is the value of t?

SOLUTION

The correct response is:

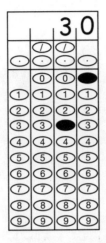

$y = 1990 - 1900 = 90$, $A = 800$, $B = 172{,}800$. Then $172{,}800 = (800)(6^{90/t})$, which simplifies to $216 = 6^{90/t}$. Since $216 = 6^{90/t}$, $3 = \frac{90}{t}$. Thus $t = 30$.

■ PROBLEM II.108

If $14nt = m$ and $3m = 2n(7^2)$ when m, n, and $t > 0$, what is the value of $3t$?

SOLUTION

The correct response is:

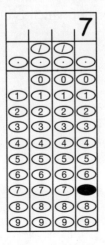

Multiplying the given equations, we get $3(14)mnt = (2m)(n)(49)$. Divide each side of this equation by $14mn$: $3t = 7$.

■ PROBLEM II.109

How many positive factors of the number $2^4 \cdot 5^2 \cdot 7^3$ are <u>not</u> divisible by 5?

SOLUTION

The correct response is:

The required factors would be in the form $2^x \cdot 7^y$, where $x = 0, 1, 2, 3, 4$, and $y = 0, 1, 2, 3$. Since we can choose any one of five different exponents for the base 2 and any one of four different exponents for the base 7, there are $(5)(4) = 20$ different possible factors, none of which is divisible by 5.

■ PROBLEM II.110

In the square $ABCD$, $OC = 3OA$. The radius of circle O is 5. What is the area of the square?

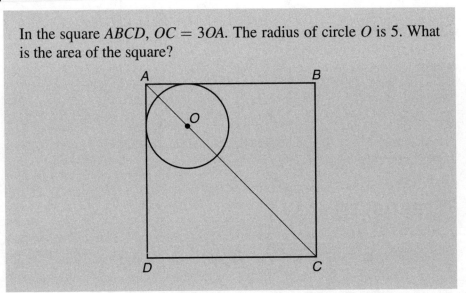

SOLUTION

The correct response is:

Since segment AC divides angle A into two equal parts, it makes ARO an isoceles right triangle. See the drawing on the following page. Then $OA = OR2.130 = 5(2.130)$. This implies $AC = 3[5(2.130)] = 15(2.130)$. Using the Pythagorean Theorem in $\triangle ABC$, $(AC)^2 = 2(AB)^2$. $[15(2.130)] = 2(AB)^2$, or $(AB)^2 = 225$. This is equal to the area of the square.

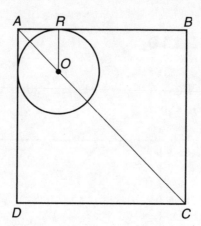

■ PROBLEM II.111

Gina drives a distance of 10 miles in 20 minutes. She then drives
the next 20 miles at 40 miles per hour. What is her average speed,
in miles per hour?

SOLUTION

The correct response is:

```
          3 6
        ⊘ ⊘
    ⊙   ⊙  ⊙   ⊙
        ⓪  ⓪   ⓪
    ①   ①  ①   ①
    ②   ②  ②   ②
    ③   ③  ●   ③
    ④   ④  ④   ④
    ⑤   ⑤  ⑤   ⑤
    ⑥   ⑥  ⑥   ●
    ⑦   ⑦  ⑦   ⑦
    ⑧   ⑧  ⑧   ⑧
    ⑨   ⑨  ⑨   ⑨
```

Her time for the first part of the trip is 20 minutes $= \frac{1}{3}$ hour. The time for the
second part of the trip is $\frac{20}{40} = \frac{1}{2}$ hour. Gina's average rate is her total distance
divided by her total time $= \frac{10+20}{\frac{1}{3}+\frac{1}{2}} = \frac{30}{\frac{5}{6}} = 36$ miles per hour.

PROBLEM II.112

Define $f(x)$ *as follows:*

$$\begin{cases} \text{when } x \leq 0, f(x) = 2x^2 \\ \text{when } x > 0, f(x) = x^2 + 2x \end{cases}$$

What is the value of $f(5) + f(-5)$?

SOLUTION

The correct response is:

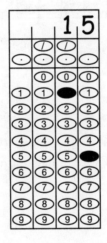

$f(5) = 5^2 + (2)(5) = 35$, and $f(-5) = (2)(-5)^2 = 50$. Thus, $f(5) + f(-5) = 85$.

PROBLEM II.113

If $a^c = 2^{-1/2}$, what is the value of $2a^{2c}$?

SOLUTION

The correct response is:

$a^{2c} = (a^c)(a^c) = (2^{-1/2})(2^{-1/2}) = 2^{-1}$. Then $2a^{2c} = (2^1)(2^{-1}) = 2^0 = 1$.

■ PROBLEM II.114

In the repeating decimal $0.\overline{021579} = 0.02157921579\ldots$, which digit lies in the 453rd place to the right of the decimal point?

SOLUTION

The correct response is:

Note that the digit 2 lies in positions 2, 7, 12, ... ; the digit 1 lies in positions 3, 8, 13, ... ; the digit 5 lies in positions 4, 9, 14, ... ; the digit 7 lies in positions 5, 10, 15, ... ; and the digit 9 lies in positions 6, 11, 16, ... To find the correct digit in the 453rd place, we divide 453 by the number of repeating digits. So $453/5 = 90$ with a remainder of 3. Then, we need to find the digit whose position corresponds to the remainder. The required digit is 1. Note that the digit 0 only appears once.

■ PROBLEM II.115

In the figure below, $\overline{AB}$ and $\overline{CD}$ are diameters of the circle. Point E is exactly halfway between points B and C, and point F is exactly halfway between points B and D. Keeping the rest of the circle stationary, if point F were rotated 628° *counter-clockwise* around the circle, in which numbered sector would F lie?

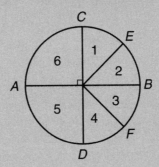

SOLUTION

The correct response is:

A rotation of 628° is equivalent to 628° − 360° = 268° of rotation. Going counter-clockwise 180° from where F is currently stationed would place this point midway between points A and C. Then the additional 268° − 180° = 88° rotation would place it almost midway between points A and D, which lies in sector 5.

PROBLEM II.116

A recipe for cake calls for $\frac{1}{3}$ cup of flour for every $1\frac{1}{4}$ teaspoons of sugar. How many teaspoons of sugar are needed if the cake requires $1\frac{2}{3}$ cups of flour?

SOLUTION

The correct response is:

Let $x =$ the required teaspoons of sugar. After converting $1\frac{1}{4}$ to $\frac{5}{4}$ and converting $1\frac{2}{3}$ to $\frac{5}{3}$, we can use the proportion $\frac{\frac{1}{3}}{\frac{5}{3}} = \frac{\frac{5}{4}}{x}$. This simplifies to $\left(\frac{1}{3}\right)(x) = \left(\frac{5}{3}\right)\left(\frac{5}{4}\right) = 2\frac{5}{12}$. Finally, $x = \left(2\frac{5}{12}\right)\left(\frac{3}{1}\right) = \frac{25}{4}$.

■ PROBLEM II.117

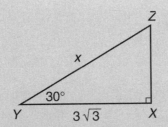

Note: Figure not drawn to scale.
In $\triangle XYZ$ shown above, what is the length of x?

SOLUTION

The correct response is:

This problem can be solved with either the Pythagorean theorem or with trigonometry. Using trigonometry, calculate cos 30x. Substitute in the value of cos 30°, which is 0.866, and solve for x. Using the Pythagorean theorem and the Special Right Triangles given in the SAT's "Reference Information" box, substitute the information given in the problem to produce the equation $(3\sqrt{3})^2 + x^2 = (2x)^2$, which gives $27 = 3x^2$. So the special triangle's $x = 3$, and the hypotenuse (x in the actual problem) $= 6$.

■ PROBLEM II.118

Define the symbol as follows:

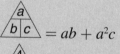

What is the value of ⟨4 5 3⟩?

SOLUTION

The correct response is:

Using the formula given, we get $(4)(5) + (4^2)(3) = 20 + 48 = 68$.

■ PROBLEM II.119

The circle shown below represents a dartboard. *MNPQ* is an inscribed square. If a dart is thrown and lands on the dartboard, what is the probability that it lands in the shaded area?

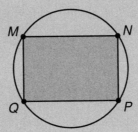

SOLUTION

The correct response is:

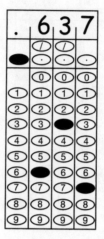

Let $1 =$ the radius of the circle. The area of the circle $= (\pi)(1^2) = \pi$. Since the diagonal of the square is a diameter of the circle, its length is 2. This means that each side of the square is 2.130. The area of the square must then be $2.130 \times 2.130 = 2$. The required probability is $2/\pi \approx .637$.

■ PROBLEM II.120

In a geometric sequence, if the fourth term is 216 and the seventh term is 64, what is the first term?

SOLUTION

The correct response is:

The formula for a geometric sequence is $L = AR^{N-1}$, where L is the missing term, A is the first term, R is the common ratio, and N is the number of terms. By substitution, we get the equations $216 = AR^3$ and $64 = AR^6$. Dividing the second equation by the first equation, we get $R^3 = \frac{64}{216}$, so $R = \frac{4}{6} = \frac{2}{3}$. Substituting into the first equation, $216 = (A)(\frac{2}{3})^3 = (A)(\frac{8}{27})$. Solving, $A = (216)(\frac{27}{8}) = 729$.

REFERENCE TABLE

SYMBOLS AND THEIR MEANINGS

=	is equal to	$\leq$	is less than or equal to
$\neq$	is unequal to	$\geq$	is greater than or equal to
<	is less than	$\parallel$	is parallel to
>	is greater than	$\perp$	is perpendicular to

FORMULAS

DESCRIPTION

FORMULA

Area (A) of a:

square $\qquad A = s^2$; where s = side

rectangle $\qquad A = lw$; where l = length, w = width

parallelogram $\qquad A = bh$; where b = base, h = height

triangle $\qquad A = \frac{1}{2} bh$; where b = base, h = height

circle $\qquad A = \pi r^2$; where π = 3.14, r = radius

Perimeter (P) of a:

square $\qquad P = 4s$; where s = side

rectangle $\qquad P = 2l + 2w$; where l = length, w = width

triangle $\qquad P = a + b + c$; where a, b, and c are the sides

circumference (C) of a circle $\quad C = \pi d$; where π = 3.14, d = diameter = $2r$

Volume (V) of a:

cube $\qquad V = s^3$; where s = side

rectangular solid $\qquad V = lwh$; where l = length, w = width, h = height

Pythagorean Theorem $\qquad c^2 = a^2 + b^2$; where c = hypotenuse, a and b are legs of a right triangle

Distance (d):

between two points in a plane

$$d = \sqrt{\left(x_2 - x_1\right)^2 + \left(y_2 - y_1\right)^2}$$

where (x_1, y_1) and (x_2, y_2) are two points in a plane

as a function of rate and time $\qquad d = rt$; where r = rate, t = time

Mean $\qquad \text{mean} = \dfrac{x_1 + x_2 + ... + x_n}{n}$

where the x's are the values for which a mean is desired, and n = number of values in the series

Median $\qquad$ median = the point in an ordered set of numbers at which half of the numbers are above and half of the numbers are below this value

Simple Interest (i) $\qquad i = prt$; where p = principal, r = rate, t = time

Total Cost (c) $\qquad c = nr$; where n = number of units, r = cost per unit

INDEX

Numbers on this page refer to PROBLEM NUMBERS, not page numbers.